CAMBRIDGE LATIN COURSE

BOOK I

CAMBRIDGE SCHOOL CLASSICS PROJECT

University Printing House, Cambridge CB2 8BS, United Kingdom

One Liberty Plaza, 20th Floor, New York, NY 10006, USA

477 Williamstown Road, Port Melbourne, VIC 3207, Australia

314–321, 3rd Floor, Plot 3, Splendor Forum, Jasola District Centre, New Delhi – 110025, India

103 Penang Road, #05–06/07, Visioncrest Commercial, Singapore 238467

Cambridge University Press is part of the University of Cambridge.

It furthers the University's mission by disseminating knowledge in the pursuit of education, learning and research at the highest international levels of excellence.

www.cambridge.org
Information on this title: www.cambridge.org/978-1-009-16264-7

First published 1970

Second edition 1982

Third edition 1990

Fourth edition 1998

Fifth edition 2022

20 19 18 17 16 15 14 13 12 11 10 9 8 7 6 5 4

Printed in Italy by L.E.G.O. S.p.A.

A catalogue record for this publication is available from the British Library

ISBN 978-1-009-16264-7 Paperback with Digital Access (5 years)

ISBN 978-1-009-16265-4 Digital Access (5 years)

Contents

Introduction

The Cambridge School Classics Project and the Cambridge Latin Course

The Cambridge School Classics Project (CSCP) is part of the Faculty of Education at the University of Cambridge and has been supporting Classics education for over fifty years. CSCP comprises a small team of Classics education and technology specialists supported by a wide community of educators and academics. All CSCP materials are based on the latest research, not only in Classics but also in language acquisition and educational theory.

While CSCP has numerous projects and initiatives supporting Classics education around the world, its first ever undertaking – the Cambridge Latin Course (CLC) – remains its most successful and influential, leading the way in evidence-based teaching of Classical languages. The underlying course structure and inductive methods of the CLC have proven effective and adaptive, responding well to the ever-changing educational environment. Most of the funding which enables CSCP's work comes from sales of the Cambridge Latin Course and associated products; therefore, every CLC purchase directly funds Classics educational research and development; grātiās!

Why study Latin with the CLC?

Languages are all about communication, and learning a language enables you to access the culture of the people who use it. Latin is no different. It may not have been the language of daily life for thousands of years, but there are many literary and historical sources about Roman life that it can still unlock.

With this in mind, the Cambridge Latin Course has two main aims:

1 to teach you to understand Latin so that you can read Latin texts confidently

2 to develop your knowledge and understanding of Roman culture, especially in the first century AD.

The course is set firmly in a Roman context, and as you study you will meet real historical characters – as well as fictional ones – and learn about the social, political and historical aspects of Roman culture.

Pay close attention not only to the text of the Latin stories and the section in English in each Stage, but also the many illustrations. These have been created or chosen to give you extra information about the Roman world and are meant to be looked at alongside the text.

How will I learn?

The CLC uses a specific approach to language learning called the 'Reading Method'. The basis of this method is, unsurprisingly, reading!

As you study with the course you will read lots of Latin stories; this is so you get used to seeing Latin in action and focusing on its meaning rather than just learning rules in isolation. The stories have been very carefully written so that you are introduced from the beginning to common Latin phrase and sentence patterns with different Latin language features woven in gradually. It is important for you to understand how the Latin words that make up a sentence or phrase actually *work*, and equally important that you get into the habit of grouping words together and trying to understand whole phrases or sentences as a single unit.

When reading the stories, you can think about how the language works and perhaps answer questions on what you understood. Afterwards, you might consider how you were able to understand what was going on, or what patterns you have noticed in the language. By the time you study a particular point of Latin language you may have seen it in action in the stories many times. You might even be able to explain how you think it works, rather than waiting for someone to tell you.

What is in my textbook?

The CLC is made up of four textbooks divided into Stages. As you work through the course, you will visit a variety of places in the Roman world: Pompeii, Roman Britain, Egypt and the city of Rome itself.

Most Stages contain new language features and all deal with a different aspect of Roman culture. The majority of them contain the following:

Model sentences

These tell a simple story using 'cartoon strips' of pictures with short sentences or paragraphs which use the new language feature you will be learning about in that Stage.

Latin stories

The stories are the main way in which you will learn about the language and get used to reading it. They get longer and more complicated as you go through the course, and new vocabulary is given alongside. You might not be able to translate every word of a story, and that's OK; the goal is for you to try to understand what is happening and get more confident at finding meaning in passages of Latin.

About the language

This section gives you an explanation of language features that have been introduced or have occurred frequently in the Stage. It usually appears some way into the Stage and is designed to be studied after you have seen the language feature in the stories, so you might have already got some idea of how it works.

Practising the language

This contains another, shorter story which uses the language feature about which you have been learning. There are questions to check your understanding and encourage you to think critically about the story and the language. This section also contains links to the places in the textbook where you can find more information on the language.

Cultural background material

This material explores an aspect of Roman culture that is important to the story line in the Stage. Each one is introduced by an **Enquiry**: a question for you to think about as you read the material. It appears again at the end of the section with bullet points highlighting what you have learnt and how this relates to the Enquiry. Throughout the material are questions, activities and discussion ideas called **Thinking points**. You may not use all of them, but they can be a good opportunity to think more closely about what you have just learned.

Vocabulary checklist

At the end of each Stage there is a list of common words which have occurred several times in the text with which you should now be familiar.

For extra help with the language, you need to check the **Language information** section at the back of the book. This is split into three sections.

Part One: About the language

This section summarises the language content of the book (and in Books II–IV the language features from previous books). It contains grammatical tables, notes and additional exercises.

Part Two: Reviewing the language

This section contains additional exercises for each Stage in the book. These exercises have been designed to help support you as you review language information – exercises are clearly labelled and numbered so that you can see your progress, and there are links to the places in the textbook where you can find additional support.

Part Three: Vocabulary

This section is where you will find the complete vocabulary for the whole book.

Time chart

Throughout this book BC and AD are used when referring to dates, as this is the system you are most likely to encounter in your wider studies of ancient history and Latin. This system was created in the sixth century AD and it uses the 'birth of Jesus Christ' as its point of reference. Many other dating systems exist and have existed over the course of human history.

An easy alternative, should you not wish to use BC and AD, is that which uses BCE (Before Common Era) and CE (Common Era). This system uses the same point of reference as BC and AD, so you can simply swap BC for BCE and AD for CE.

Date	Pompeii	The Roman World	The Wider World
BC			
2500–1500			c.2500: Great Pyramid at Giza completed in Egypt; Stonehenge built in England
			c.2300: Babylon founded
			c.2000–1200: Epic of Gilgamesh created in Mesopotamia
			c.1750: Babylonian king Hammurabi proclaims one of the earliest written legal codes
			c.1600: Minoan civilisation at its height; evidence of a fully developed writing system in China
1500–500	c.700–600: Greek merchants settle in what was probably an older Oscan community c.530: Etruscans control Pompeii	753: Traditional date of the foundation of Rome 509: Kings expelled; beginning of the Roman Republic 508: Roman–Etruscan Wars	c.1000–800: Phoenician alphabet adapted by the Greeks; Homer's *Iliad* and *Odyssey* orally composed 776: Traditional date of the first Olympic games c.720: Building begins on the largest group of Nubian pyramids at Meroë c.563–c.483: Suggested dates for the life of Siddhartha Gautama (The Buddha) 522–486: Persian Empire at its greatest extent; first attempted Persian invasion of Greece 508: Cleisthenes establishes the foundations of the Athenian democratic system
500–300	474: Samnites capture Pompeii	450: The Law of the 12 Tables: foundation of Roman Law 390: Gauls sack Rome 343–304: First and Second Samnite and Latin Wars	399: Death of Greek philosopher Socrates 335–323: Conquests of Alexander the Great
300–200	c.290: Pompeii becomes one of the *socii* (allies) bound to Rome by treaty	298–290: Third Samnite War: Romans control the whole Italian peninsula 264–241: First Punic War 218–201: Second Punic War	c.268–232: Almost all of the Indian subcontinent united under Emperor Ashoka the Great 221: China unified under First Emperor Qin Shi Huang
c.200	Temple of Isis built	Rome controls all of Italy	Compass invented in China
200–100		192–188: War with the Seleucid Empire in Greece and Asia Minor 146: Third Punic War ends with destruction of Carthage	165: Judas Maccabaeus leads the Jewish defence against the Seleucid king and restores the Temple of Jerusalem (commemorated by the festival Hanukkah) 141–87: Reign of Chinese Emperor Wu; 'Silk Road' established connecting China via Asia to Europe until the eighteenth century

Date	Pompeii	The Roman World	The Wider World
BC			
100–70	91–89: Pompeii joins the Italians in the Social War; afterwards given Roman citizenship; Latin replaces Oscan as official language 80: Pompeii probably becomes a Roman colony	91–89: Social War 88–79: Sulla's first civil war and dictatorship 73: Spartacus' uprising	90–70: Probable date of the oldest extant Buddhist paintings found in the Ajanta Caves, India
70–50		60: Political alliance of Pompey, Julius Caesar and Crassus 58–50: Caesar's Gallic Wars 55 and 54: Caesar's first and second invasions of Britain	53: Birth of Chinese poet Yang Xiong
50–40		49–45: Civil war between Caesar and Pompey 44: Julius Caesar assassinated 43: Triumvirate of Octavian, Mark Antony and Lepidus established	48: Ptolemy XIII deposes his co-ruler and sister Cleopatra 47: Cleopatra restored to the throne
40–1	15: Major public works programme	31: Octavian defeats Mark Antony and Cleopatra at the Battle of Actium 30: Province of Egypt organised 27: Octavian given the title 'Augustus' and becomes the first emperor	30: Cleopatra, final Ptolemaic ruler of Egypt, takes her own life; By this point the Mayan civilisation has developed a symbol for zero 27: Amanirenas the Kushite Queen leads armies against the Romans
AD			
1–20		14: Death of Augustus; Tiberius becomes emperor	c.1: Beginning of explosive growth which leads to Teotihuacan becoming the largest settlement in Mesoamerica c.4: Birth of Jesus; Traditional date for the foundation of the Ise Grand Shrine in Japan
20–30		26: Pontius Pilate made governor of Judea	28: Beginning of the reign of Emperor Ming during which Buddhism traditionally reaches China
30–40		37: Death of Tiberius; Caligula becomes emperor	c.30–33: Sugested date of the crucifixion of Jesus 39–40: The Trung sisters begin their rebellion against Chinese rule in Vietnam
40–50		41: Caligula assassinated; Claudius becomes emperor 43: Initial phase of Roman conquest of Britain	43: The Trung sisters' rebellion is defeated by Chinese forces
50–60	59: Riot at the Pompeian amphitheatre	54: Death of Claudius; Nero becomes emperor	c.50: Death of Jewish philosopher Philo of Alexandria
60–70	62–63: Earthquake damages Pompeii 69: Beginning of the restoration of the amphitheatre	60–61: Boudica's revolt 64: Great fire of Rome 69: Year of the Four Emperors; Galba, Otho, Vitellius, Vespasian	68: China's first Buddhist temple, White Horse Temple, is built
70–80	79 Final elections held in March; Eruption of Vesuvius	70: Siege of Jerusalem; Second Temple destroyed 73: Siege of Masada 79: Death of Vespasian; Titus becomes emperor	78: The beginning of the Saka Era used in traditional Indian calendars

CAECILIUS

Stage 1

familia

1 Caecilius est pater.

2 Metella est māter.

3 Quīntus est fīlius.

4 Lūcia est fīlia.

5 Clēmēns est servus.

6 Grumiō est coquus.

7 Cerberus est canis.

8 Caecilius est in tablīnō.

9 Metella est in ātriō.

10 Quīntus est in trīclīniō.

11 Lūcia est in hortō.

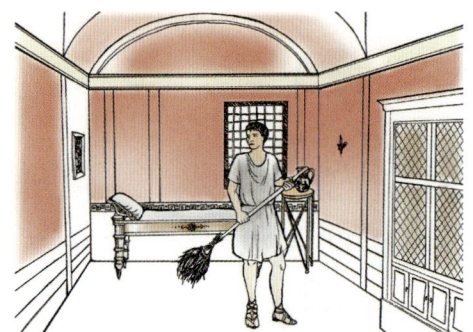

12 Clēmēns est in cubiculō.

13 Grumiō est in culīnā.

14 Cerberus est in viā.

15 pater est in tablīnō.
pater in tablīnō scrībit.

16 māter est in ātriō.
māter in ātriō sedet.

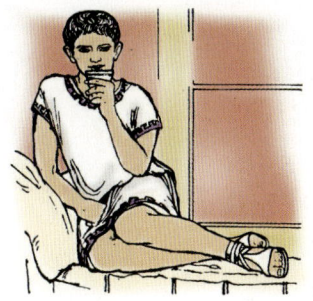

17 fīlius est in trīclīniō.
fīlius in trīclīniō bibit.

18 fīlia est in hortō.
fīlia in hortō legit.

19 servus est in cubiculō.
servus in cubiculō labōrat.

20 coquus est in culīnā.
coquus in culīnā labōrat.

21 canis est in viā.
canis in viā dormit.

Vocabulary

familia	*household*	**in tablīnō**	*in the study*	**scrībit**	*is writing*
est	*is*	**in ātriō**	*in the atrium*	**sedet**	*is sitting*
pater	*father*	**in trīclīniō**	*in the dining*	**bibit**	*is drinking*
māter	*mother*		*room*	**legit**	*is reading*
fīlius	*son*	**in hortō**	*in the garden*	**labōrat**	*is working*
fīlia	*daughter*	**in cubiculō**	*in the bedroom*	**dormit**	*is sleeping*
servus	*(male) slave*	**in culīnā**	*in the kitchen*		
coquus	*cook*	**in viā**	*in the street*		
canis	*dog*				

Cerberus

Caecilius est in hortō. Caecilius in hortō sedet. Lūcia est in hortō. Lūcia in hortō scrībit. Metella est in ātriō. Metella in ātriō legit. Quīntus est in tablīnō. Quīntus in tablīnō scrībit. Cerberus est in viā.

Caecilius had this mosaic of a dog in the doorway of his house.

Grumiō est in culīnā. coquus in culīnā dormit. Cerberus intrat. Cerberus circumspectat. cibus est in mēnsā. canis salit. canis in mēnsā stat. Grumiō stertit. canis lātrat. Grumiō surgit. coquus est īrātus. 'pestis! furcifer!' coquus clāmat. Cerberus exit.

5

intrat *enters*
circumspectat *looks round*
cibus *food*
in mēnsā *on the table*
salit *jumps*
stat *stands*
stertit *snores*
lātrat *barks*
surgit *gets up*
īrātus *angry*
pestis! *pest!*
furcifer! *scoundrel!*
clāmat *shouts*
exit *goes out*

About the language

1   Latin sentences containing the word **est** often have the same order as English.
    For example:

    Metella est māter.   canis est in viā.
    Metella is the mother.   *The dog is in the street.*

2   In other Latin sentences, the order is usually different from that of English.
    For example:

    canis in viā dormit.   Lūcia in hortō legit.
    The dog is sleeping in the street.   *Lucia is reading in the garden.*

3   Note that **dormit** and **legit** in the sentences above can be translated in another way.
    For example: **canis in viā dormit** can mean *The dog sleeps in the street* as well as
    The dog is sleeping in the street. The story will help you to decide which translation
    gives the better sense.

Reviewing the language Stage 1: page 222

This stove and the bronze cooking pots on top of it were found in the kitchen of the House of the Vettii in Pompeii. The pots would have been placed on braziers over a small fire and firewood was stored in the alcove you can see underneath.

Caecilius and his familia

The stories in the CLC might be fictional, but Caecilius was a real man who lived with his **familia** during the first century AD in the town of Pompeii in Italy. The town was situated at the foot of Mount Vesuvius on the coast of the Bay of Naples and may have had a population of between 8000 and 12 000 people including those from all over the Roman Empire.

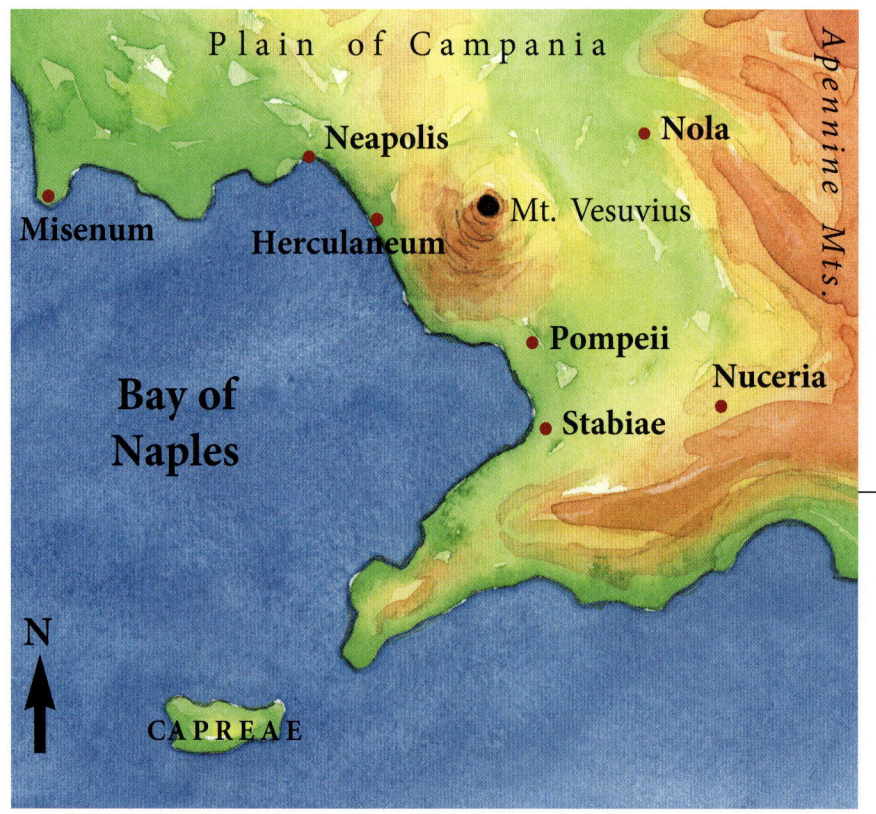

The Bay of Naples (Neapolis). The area covered by this map is about 60 kilometres (40 miles) wide.

Central and southern Italy.

A Roman familia was not a 'family' as we might think of one today. It included all the people who were part of the extended household; for example, any enslaved people they owned, or people with social ties and obligations to the family. The oldest living male in the familia was its legal head and referred to as the **paterfamiliās**.

Archaeologists study human history by uncovering and analysing the physical remains left by people who lived in the past. When Caecilius' house was excavated they discovered his business accounts written on tablets in a wooden chest. These revealed that Caecilius was a rich Pompeian citizen whose work included acting as an auctioneer, tax collector and moneylender. He may have owned a few shops as well.

The front of Caecilius' house. The spaces on either side of the door were shops he probably owned.

One of the wooden tablets found in Caecilius' house. The writing would have been on wax in the central recess. The wax disappeared long ago, but the stylus had scratched through it and marked the wood beneath, meaning much of the writing could still be read. The tablets were tied together in twos or threes through the holes at the top.

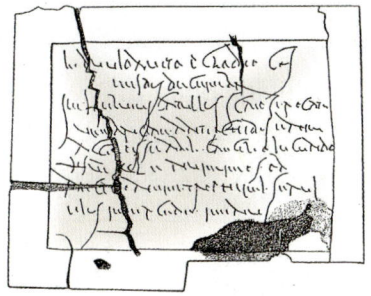

A re-creation of one of the tablets: it records the sale at auction of an enslaved man named Trophimus for 6252 sesterces. Caecilius handled this sale on behalf of a woman named Umbricia.

Caecilius kept his tablets and money in a wooden chest, which may have looked a bit like this wood and metal strongbox.

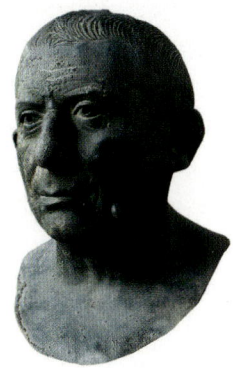

This head found in Caecilius' house may be a portrait of him, although some historians think it might actually be his father.

> **Thinking point 1:** What can we learn about Caecilius from these items? What can't we learn from them?

Throughout the course you will be guided through the information about the Roman world by characters from the stories. While what these characters 'say' is fictional, their words are based on evidence and reflect what modern historians think the Roman world was like. Here we imagine Caecilius explaining how he has become so wealthy:

> While I inherited some of my money, I made most of it through my business activities. I trade in enslaved people, cloth, timber and property. I also run a laundry and dyeing business, graze sheep and cattle on pastureland outside the town, and on occasion am appointed to collect the local taxes. Sometimes I lend money to local shipping companies wishing to trade overseas. The profit on sea-trading like this is often very large.

Thinking point 2: Caecilius lists human beings alongside cloth, timber and property as 'items' he trades; what Roman attitude towards enslaved people does this reflect?

Caecilius' full name was Lucius Caecilius Iucundus. Lucius was his personal name, rather like a modern first name. His second name, Caecilius, shows that he was a member of the 'clan' of the Caecilii. Clans or groups of families were very important and strong feelings of loyalty existed within them. Caecilius' third name, Iucundus, is the name of his own family and close relatives. The word **iūcundus** means 'pleasant', just as in English we find surnames like Merry or Jolly.

> Only Roman citizens like Caecilius have three names. Enslaved people have only one; I am just 'Grumio'. Usually we are stripped of our original name very soon after being enslaved. I can't remember mine; I was very young when I was first sold. Our names can be changed on the whim of the person whose property we are considered to be.
>
> As a Roman citizen, Caecilius can vote in elections and is fully protected by the law against unjust treatment. The enslaved people who live and work in his house and businesses, however, do not have these rights. We are regarded as his property and he can treat us as he likes.

Metella

There is much less evidence available from the Roman world about women than there is about men. For example, we know that Caecilius had at least two sons, Quintus and Sextus, but we do not know anything about their mother. We have therefore imagined the character of Metella. A woman like Metella may have had ten or twelve children, only some of whom would have survived to adulthood. For our stories we have also given the family a daughter, Lucia.

Roman girls are traditionally named after their father's clan. My name indicates that I was born into the clan of the Metelli. Sisters are distinguished by the addition of a second name, sometimes taken from a family member. As a daughter of Caecilius, my daughter's full name is Caecilia Lucia; however, she prefers simply to be called 'Lucia'.

As women, Lucia and I do not have the same rights and control over our lives as Caecilius and Quintus. These days, the law gives most fathers (or another man who is acting as paterfamilias) control over their daughters, even after a daughter is married.

Roman girls like Lucia would usually have been married before they were 20, often to a man chosen by their paterfamilias. Arranged marriages were also used to create links between rich and powerful families, and to ensure that there would be heirs to any property and influence. Daughters in these upper-class families could be married as young as 12. Although Roman law required a woman's consent for her marriage to be valid, it must have been difficult for many women and girls to go against the wishes of their family.

In the Roman world, however, households took many different forms. Plenty had informal arrangements which did not involve a legal ceremony and not all were centred on a marriage between a man and a woman. While the community may have recognised all these arrangements as the basis for a legitimate household, they probably did not all share the same status under Roman law.

> **Thinking point 3:** What claims can we make about the status of Roman women compared with Roman men based on
> a) Roman names and b) Roman marriage customs?

Houses in Pompeii

Thinking point 4: Think back to the sentences at the beginning of the Stage and the story you have read; what do you already know about Caecilius' house?

The house of someone wealthy like Caecilius would have differed considerably from the homes of most people living in Pompeii. Some of the poorer shopkeepers, for instance, would have had only a room or two above their shops. In large cities such as Rome, many people lived in apartment buildings several stories high, sometimes in very poor conditions. Pompeian neighbourhoods contained a variety of houses and buildings. On the same block as Caecilius' house were many shops with accommodation attached, a number of bars and a laundry, as well as other houses of different sizes.

Houses came right up to the pavement; there was no garden or grass in front of them. The outsides were plastered and painted and the windows were few, small and fairly high up. The windows were intended to let in some light but keep out the heat of the sun. Most windows had no glass but many had iron grilles in them for security. Some houses had a second floor and many had shops on either side that were rented out by the owner of the house. Front doors of houses may have been left open to encourage passers-by to peer in.

Many features of Roman houses are described on this page. Which ones can you find in these pictures of houses in Pompeii?

Thinking point 5: Why do you think wealthy Romans might have encouraged passers-by to peer into their houses?

Plan of a Pompeian house

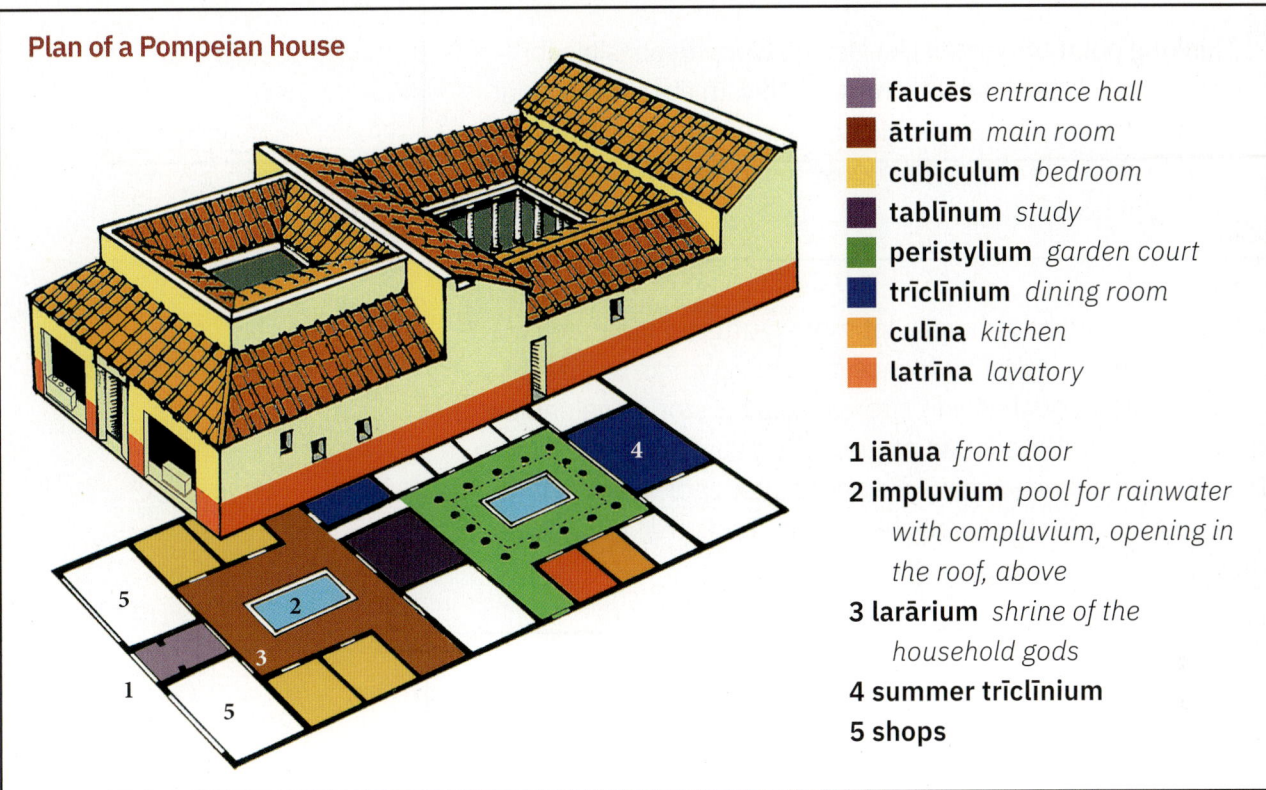

- **faucēs** *entrance hall*
- **ātrium** *main room*
- **cubiculum** *bedroom*
- **tablīnum** *study*
- **peristylium** *garden court*
- **trīclīnium** *dining room*
- **culīna** *kitchen*
- **latrīna** *lavatory*

1 iānua *front door*
2 impluvium *pool for rainwater with compluvium, opening in the roof, above*
3 larārium *shrine of the household gods*
4 summer trīclīnium
5 shops

Houses have their main entrance – a tall double door (**iānua**) – on the side facing the street leading straight into the main room, the **ātrium**. The atrium is used for important family occasions and for receiving visitors, so it's usually quite impressive. The floor might be paved with marble slabs or sometimes with mosaics. The walls are decorated with panels of brightly painted plaster. Pompeians are especially fond of red, orange and blue. Many people have scenes from well-known stories, especially the Greek myths, painted on these panels. Most houses have a small shrine (**larārium**) in the atrium at which the family gods (**Larēs**) are worshipped. Ours is in a corner near the main door.

The roof over the atrium slopes down slightly towards a large square opening called the **compluvium**. Light streams in through this opening, as does rainwater that is collected in the **impluvium** (a shallow rectangular pool) directly below. The atrium feels so big with its high roof and glimpse of the sky through the compluvium.

Around the atrium are the bedrooms, study and dining room. These rooms can have more than one function; for example, sometimes bedrooms are used for private business meetings.

A lararium.

Thinking point 6: Women like Metella were responsible for keeping the household running smoothly. In the sentences at the beginning of this Stage, Metella is seen sitting in the atrium. Why do you think she might choose to sit here? What activities might she be doing?

Houses would have been a lot more cluttered than their remains might suggest. Evidence of items such as bronze or marble tables, couches and strongboxes for storing valuables, all common furniture for an atrium, often survived the eruption. There would, however, have also been plenty of wooden furniture like chests, cupboards, wall shelves and beds that did not survive.

Thinking point 7: Make a note of what types of evidence generally did and did not survive the volcanic eruption which destroyed Pompeii. Why do you think this is the case?

The atrium in Caecilius' house as it is today (above, left). We can see how spacious it was, but for a real sense of how impressive an atrium might be we need to look at a better-preserved one (above, right). The visitor entering the front door would see, beyond the impluvium, the tablinum and the sunlit peristylium.

From this first area of the house, you can walk through the **tablīnum** (study) into the second part, the **peristȳlium**. This is made up of a covered area supported by columns (colonnade) surrounding the **hortus** (garden). Like the atrium, the colonnade is often elaborately decorated and designed to provide shade. It also encourages breezes to waft through the house to keep it cool; Pompeii is so hot in summer! Around the outside of the colonnade are the summer **trīclīnium** (dining room), **culīna** (kitchen), lavatory, storage rooms and living quarters for enslaved people. Some people even have a set of baths in their house! Our house isn't grand enough for that, though.

> **Thinking point 8:** Where is the tablinum located in the house? What does this tell us about how it was used?

Caecilius' tablinum was decorated with vibrant colours, including a particularly expensive shade of red paint, and looked out onto the garden.

![Caecilius' garden with reconstructed formal planting. You can also see the columns of the peristylium.](photo)

Caecilius' garden with reconstructed formal planting. You can also see the columns of the peristylium.

Our garden is laid out with flowers and shrubs in a careful plan. There's a small fishpond in the middle with a fountain which throws up a jet of water. There are also marble statues of gods and heroes here and there. The peristylium is a nice place to enjoy the sunshine — or shade!

The work of Dr Wilhelmina Jashemski showed that almost every building in Pompeii had one or more gardens. She uncovered everything from working farms densely planted with vines and fruit trees, to small household vegetable patches, to formal gardens in luxury villas. Scientists working with Dr Jashemski identified the plants using ancient pollen, seeds, fruit or stems and even casts of the root systems.

This vineyard is part of a project aiming to recreate the wines of ancient Pompeii. Working with archaeologists to excavate the sites, study ancient wall paintings and test the DNA of the ancient vines, the winemakers have replanted these vineyards using the same grape varieties and techniques as the Romans.

Thinking point 9: What did the Romans use their gardens for? How is this similar or different from today?

A house is not a private place just for family and close friends. I conduct much of my business and social life from home. I receive most visitors in the atrium and stay there to do business. I might ask more important people to join me in the tablinum. Certain very close business friends and high-ranking individuals might be invited to dine in one of my dining rooms or to relax in the peristylium with the family.

Even if there were no outsiders present, the members of the family were never on their own. They were surrounded and often outnumbered by the enslaved people who worked in the house.

Thinking point 10: What do you think are the biggest differences between Caecilius' house and a modern home?

Enquiry: Who was Lucius Caecilius Iucundus and what claims can we make about him and his household?

You may wish to consider the following:

- what we know about Caecilius as a person, for example, his family and his home
- the evidence we have to support these claims
- what we don't know about Caecilius and his household
- the assumptions we can make based on what we know about typical Roman life.

Vocabulary checklist 1

canis	*dog*
coquus	*cook*
est	*is*
fīlia	*daughter*
fīlius	*son*
hortus	*garden*
in	*in*
labōrat	*works, is working*
māter	*mother*
pater	*father*
servus	*(male) slave*
via	*street*

Wall painting of birds around a marble fountain found in the garden of the House of Venus in the Shell.

amīcus

1 Caecilius est in ātriō.

2 amīcus Caecilium salūtat.

3 Metella est in ātriō.

4 amīcus Metellam salūtat.

5 fīlius est in ātriō.

6 amīcus fīlium salūtat.

7 fīlia est in ātriō.

8 amīcus fīliam salūtat.

9 canis est in ātriō.

10 amīcus canem salūtat.

Metella

11 coquus est in culīnā.

12 Metella culīnam intrat.

13 Grumiō labōrat.

14 Metella Grumiōnem spectat.

15 cibus est pāvō.

16 Metella cibum gustat.

17 Grumiō est anxius.

18 Metella Grumiōnem laudat.

19 amīcus est in hortō.

20 Metella amīcum vocat.

mercātor

amīcus Caecilium vīsitat. amīcus est Barbillus. Barbillus est mercātor. mercātor vīllam intrat.

Clēmēns est in ātriō. Clēmēns mercātōrem salūtat. Caecilius est in tablīnō. Caecilius pecūniam numerat. Caecilius est argentārius. amīcus tablīnum intrat. Caecilius surgit.

'salvē!' Caecilius mercātōrem salūtat.

'salvē!' mercātor respondet.

Caecilius trīclīnium intrat. Barbillus quoque intrat. amīcus in lectō recumbit. argentārius in lectō recumbit.

Grumiō in culīnā cantat. Grumiō pāvōnem coquit. coquus est laetus. Caecilius coquum audit. Caecilius nōn est laetus. Caecilius cēnam exspectat. amīcus cēnam exspectat. Caecilius Grumiōnem vocat.

mercātor	*merchant*
amīcus	*friend*
vīsitat	*is visiting*
vīllam	*house*
salūtat	*greets*
pecūniam numerat	
	is counting money
argentārius	*banker*
salvē!	*hello!*
respondet	*replies*
quoque	*also*
in lectō recumbit	
	reclines on a couch
cantat	*is singing*
pāvōnem coquit	
	is cooking peacock
laetus	*happy*
audit	*hears, listens to*
nōn est	*is not*
cēnam exspectat	
	is waiting for dinner
vocat	*calls*

5

10

in trīclīniō

Grumiō trīclīnium intrat. Grumiō pāvōnem portat. Clēmēns trīclīnium intrat. Clēmēns vīnum portat. Caecilius pāvōnem gustat.

'pāvō est optimus!' Caecilius clāmat.

mercātor quoque pāvōnem gustat. cēna Barbillum dēlectat. dominus coquum laudat. Grumiō exit.

ancilla intrat. ancilla est Poppaea. Poppaea suāviter cantat. dominus Poppaeam audit et vīnum bibit. mox dominus dormit. amīcus quoque dormit.

Grumiō trīclīnium intrat et circumspectat. coquus cibum in mēnsā videt. Grumiō cibum cōnsūmit et vīnum bibit. Caecilius Grumiōnem nōn videt. coquus in trīclīniō magnificē cēnat.

Poppaea coquum spectat. coquus ancillam vocat. Poppaea cibum gustat et Grumiōnem laudat. Grumiō est laetissimus.

portat	*is carrying*
vīnum	*wine*
gustat	*tastes*
optimus	*very good, excellent*
dēlectat	*pleases*
dominus	*master*
laudat	*praises*
ancilla	*(female) slave*
suāviter	*sweetly*
et	*and*
mox	*soon*
videt	*sees*
cōnsūmit	*eats*
magnificē	
	impressively, magnificently
cēnat	*dines, has dinner*
spectat	*looks at*
laetissimus	*very happy*

5

10

About the language

1 Words like **Metella**, **Caecilius** and **mercātor** are known as **nouns**. They often indicate people or animals (e.g. **fīlia**, **canis**), places (e.g. **vīlla**, **hortus**) and things (e.g. **cēna**, **cibus**).

2 You have now met two forms of the same noun:

Metella – Metellam
Caecilius – Caecilium
mercātor – mercātōrem

3 The different forms are known as the **nominative case** and the **accusative case**.

| *nominative* | Metella | Caecilius | mercātor |
| *accusative* | Metellam | Caecilium | mercātōrem |

4 If Metella does something, such as greeting Grumio, the nominative **Metella** is used:

Metella Grumiōnem salūtat.
Metella greets Grumio.

5 But if somebody else does something to Metella, the accusative **Metellam** is used:

amīcus **Metellam** salūtat.
The friend greets Metella.

6 Notice again the difference in word order between Latin and English:

Metella culīnam intrat.
Metella enters the kitchen.

Caecilius pecūniam numerat.
Caecilius is counting money.

Peacocks often featured on Pompeian wall paintings as well as occasionally on their dinner tables.

Practising the language

in culīnā

Grumio finds an uninvited guest in the kitchen.

amīcus Grumiōnem vīsitat. amīcus est Corvus. amīcus
vīllam intrat. Clēmēns est in ātriō. Corvus Clēmentem
videt. Clēmēns Corvum salūtat. amīcus culīnam intrat.
amīcus culīnam circumspectat.

   Grumiō nōn est in culīnā. Corvus cibum videt. cibus   5
est parātus! Corvus cibum gustat. cibus est optimus.

   Grumiō culīnam intrat. Grumiō amīcum videt. amicus cibum
cōnsūmit! coquus est īrātus.

   'pestis! furcifer!' coquus clāmat. coquus amīcum vituperat.

parātus *ready*

vituperat *rebukes*

---

1 **Explore the story**

  a **amīcus Grumiōnem vīsitat. amīcus est Corvus** (line 1): what two things are we told about the friend?

  b **Corvus Clēmentem videt. Clēmēns Corvum salūtat** (lines 2–3): what happens after Corvus sees Clemens?

  c **Grumiō nōn est in culīnā. Corvus cibum videt. cibus est parātus! Corvus cibum gustat. cibus est optimus** (lines 5–6): which two of the following statements are true?

     A Grumio is in the kitchen.   **C** Corvus tastes the food.

     B The food is not ready.   **D** The food is very good.

  d **Grumiō culīnam intrat. Grumiō amīcum videt** (line 7): what two things does Grumio do?

  e **amīcus cibum cōnsūmit! coquus est īrātus** (lines 7–8): why is the cook angry?

  f **'pestis! furcifer!' coquus clāmat. coquus amīcum vituperat** (line 9): what does the cook say as he rebukes his friend?

2 **Explore the language**

Explain why **Clēmēns** and **Clēmentem** (lines 2–3) have different endings.

nominative case and **accusative case**: page 25

3 **Explore further**

Think about the whole of this story and the other stories you have read in this stage. Grumio, Poppaea and Corvus are very hungry and take food wherever they can find it. How different is this to Caecilius' and Barbillus' experience of food and eating?

Reviewing the language Stage 2: page 223

Daily life in Caecilius' household

Daily life in Caecilius' household would have been shaped by the expectations and privileges of his status as a wealthy man. Life for most people living in Pompeii at that time would have been very different. Most people would have had a trade, and the majority of their time would have been taken up by work. Caecilius also owned many enslaved people, some of whom would have done the housework under the watchful eye of Metella. Poorer households might also have owned enslaved people but they would have had far fewer, so members of the family would have done more household chores and work themselves.

An important Roman dressed in his toga. Only male citizens were allowed to wear the toga, and the type of toga someone wore reflected his social status.

> **Thinking point 1:** Think about the stories and cultural background material you have read and the pictures you have seen. What do you already know about daily life in Caecilius' household?

My family and I get up at dawn. I don't eat much for breakfast, just a light snack like a piece of bread and a cup of water.

Then I get dressed in a long shirt with short sleeves (**tunica**) and my **toga**. Putting the toga on is a two-person job, as it is a very large, heavy piece of woollen cloth arranged in a series of complex folds. Finally, I put on my shoes. A quick wash of my hands and face with cold water is enough first thing in the morning; later I'll visit a barber and be shaved and maybe take a leisurely trip to the public baths.

> **Thinking point 2:** Look at the statue of a Roman wearing a toga and think about Caecilius' description of getting dressed. What do you think it would be like to wear one for a day? Why do you think male Roman citizens went to the trouble of wearing them?

I get up and dress in a **stola**, a full-length tunic that is usually worn over the top of another tunic. If I'm going out I wear a **palla,** a large rectangular shawl which can be worn on my head to cover my hair. I wear my hair in the latest fashion, use whitening powder to lighten my skin, and apply blusher and eyeliner. Finally, I arrange my jewellery.

Thinking point 3: Why do you think Roman women a) wore the palla over their heads and b) used powder to whiten their skin?

A Roman woman wearing a stola and palla.

Wealthy women's hairstyles were often very elaborate, and were often created and maintained by a highly skilled enslaved hairdresser known as an ornatrix.

Examples of jewellery a rich woman like Metella might have owned.

By the time dawn arrives the enslaved members of the household have usually been up for hours preparing for the day. Getting washed and dressed is very quick – no toga or fancy hairstyles for me. What little sleep I get is in the kitchen where I work; it's small, dark, hot, smokey and smelly. Sometimes I sit on the steps outside and do things like prepare vegetables so I can have some fresh air. I'm expected to help keep watch and guard the doorway when I do, though.

After breakfast I go to the atrium for the **salūtātiō**, the respectful greetings of my **clientēs** (clients), a number of poorer people and freedmen, some of whom were previously enslaved members of my household. I am their **patrōnus** (patron), which means I do things like offer them small sums of money and try to help and protect them if they are in trouble. In return, my clients must do things for me. For example, they accompany me as a group of supporters on public occasions and I employ some of them in my business activities.

After receiving my clients, if I have no further business to conduct at home, I set out for the **forum**, where I spend the rest of the morning making deals and banking.

Lunch is another light meal, perhaps bread with meat or fish followed by fruit. Business ends soon after lunch and then it's time for a nap before going to the baths.

Thinking point 4: What do you think was the purpose of the salutatio? How did both the clients and the patron benefit from this relationship? Do you think they benefited equally?

The outside of the House of Menander. On either side of the door are stone benches; it has been suggested that these were for clients to sit on while waiting to greet their patron.

I enjoy doing things like reading and weaving at home, or going out to shop, visit friends or visit the baths, but I am responsible for the management of the whole household, and that keeps me very busy. I supervise the enslaved people who work in the house and manage the household finances. To run a successful household a woman needs to be able to read and write and be well organised.

I am trying to teach Lucia everything she'll need to know when she has her own household to run. I also make sure she understands what's expected of a Roman woman in terms of her behaviour and manners.

A wealthy woman like Metella may not have worked outside the home, but in other households women might make important contributions to the finances by weaving and spinning thread or wool and being involved in the family business. It was unusual for women to manage their own businesses, but widows sometimes took control of their late husbands' business affairs. Women did a range of jobs including being midwives, makers of cloth or gold jewellery, barbers, medical doctors, scribes, or sellers of various goods such as silk, perfumes and fish. We have evidence about many women who lived in Pompeii whose lives may have been very different from Metella's, for example:

- Julia Felix rented out property and owned a bar, restaurant and bath complex.
- Asellina owned a bar and supported some political candidates.
- Eumachia was a priestess of the cult of the emperor, patron of the cloth-workers (fullers) and an important benefactor. She financed construction of one of the largest buildings in Pompeii.
- Naevoleia Tyche was a women freed from enslavement who probably became wealthy through overseas trade using ships.

Thinking point 5: Based on the descriptions of Caecilius and Metella in Stages 1 and 2, which character's daily life is more appealing to you? Why?

Thinking point 6: How typical of Roman women do you think the character of Metella is?

Fresco of a female shopkeeper standing behind her wooden counter with shoes on it while a customer sits and talks with her. From the façade of the House of the Fullers of M. Vecilius Verecundus.

Roman dinner parties

Towards the end of the afternoon, the main meal of the day (**cēna**) begins, although I've usually been preparing it all day (longer if it's a special occasion). A formal dinner party takes place in a dining room (triclinium), but often the family eat informally in other rooms or sitting in the garden. During the winter, dinners might be held in the inner dining room near the atrium. In the summer Caecilius generally prefers the dining room at the back of the house looking straight out onto the garden. Most people don't even have one triclinium in their house, let alone two, so they will only eat in one if they are invited to a formal dinner party elsewhere.

In the dining room three couches are arranged around a small, elegant circular table. Three guests can recline on each couch. Diners lean on their left elbow, take food from the table with their right hand and eat using their fingers or a spoon. Poorer families only recline to eat at festivals or public holidays; children and enslaved people eat sitting upright. These days women like me recline with the men, but there was a time when it wasn't very respectable to do so.

The 'low' couch is where the host reclines with either their family or more important guests. The guest of honour sits directly on the host's left on the 'middle' couch, as this is the best position for chatting with the host. Other high-status guests sit on this couch, while the least prestigious positions are on the 'high' couch. For special occasions I might organise some form of entertainment such as singers, dancers or a poetry recital.

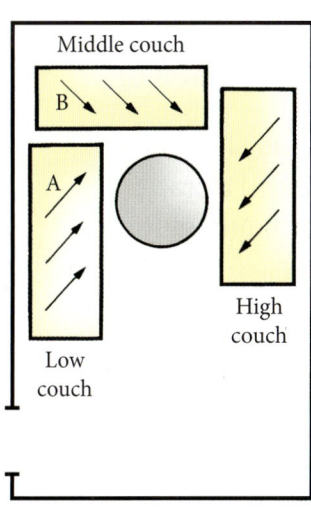

Middle couch

B

A

Low couch

High couch

Thinking point 7: Look at the diagram showing the arrangement of the couches. Where would Caecilius have been seated? What position might a good friend be given? If she attended, where might Metella be?

These drawings show how the couches were arranged in a Roman dining room. The Latin name triclinium means a room with three couches. The arrows show the position of the people eating dinner. Position A is where the host would lie, and B marks the top position of honour.

Enslaved people don't attend dinner parties; we work at them. When the guests arrive one of us will wash their feet. I prepare the food in the kitchen and it is cut up before it is served. While the guests recline and enjoy the food, we sit on the floor or stand out of the way ready to do anything that is asked of us.

Preparing a meal for an important dinner party can take me all day, and Metella pays especially close attention if important people are coming; if she doesn't like what I have prepared, I can get into terrible trouble.

A dinner party begins with light dishes, for example, eggs, fish – you can get good shellfish in Pompeii because we're so near the coast – and cooked and raw vegetables. Then comes the main course of various meat and fish dishes accompanied by sauces and vegetables. I use a lot of the local fish sauce (**garum**); Pompeii is famous for it. Pork, beef, mutton and poultry are all popular, and when preparing them I try to show off my skill and imagination. I was really pleased with the peacock for today's dinner, and relieved that Metella and the guests liked it too. Dessert consists of fruit, nuts, cheese and sweet dishes.

Wine is drunk throughout the meal, usually mixed with water. The local wine from the vineyards on the side of the mountain to the north of the town is really good, but there's also a lot available that has been imported from all over the world.

Items of food and drink often feature in the wall paintings and mosaics found in Pompeian houses – for example, this mosaic of sea creatures, and these wall paintings of a rabbit and chicken hanging in a larder and a bowl of fruit.

Some Roman authors complain about dinner party hosts who give guests different food depending on their status.

'I came to be dining ... with a man who thought he combined elegance with economy, but who appeared to me to be both mean and lavish, for he set the best dishes before himself and a few others and treated the rest to cheap and scrappy food.'

(Pliny, Letter 2.6)

'See now that huge lobster being served to my lord, all garnished with asparagus ... Before you is placed a crab hemmed in by half an egg on a tiny plate; a fit banquet for the dead.'

(Juvenal, Satire 5)

The fact that several authors mention this may imply it was a common practice. These sources are highly critical of such hosts, however, so it may not have been regarded as good manners.

> **Thinking point 8:** Why might some hosts have given different food to different guests?

Dining scene from the House of the Triclinium showing couches, soft furnishings, enslaved people (the smaller figures) and someone clearly not feeling very well!

Enquiry: How did Caecilius', Metella's and Grumio's daily activities reflect and reinforce their social status?

You may wish to consider the following:

- how they dressed
- how they spent their time
- clients and patrons
- Roman dinner parties
- comparisons which can be made between them.

Vocabulary checklist 2

amīcus	*friend*
ancilla	*(female) slave*
cēna	*dinner*
cibus	*food*
dominus	*master*
dormit	*sleeps*
intrat	*enters*
laetus	*happy*
laudat	*praises*
mercātor	*merchant*
quoque	*also*
salūtat	*greets*

Most cooking was done in the kitchen with pans and grills over charcoal, like a barbecue.

in forō

in forō *in the forum*

Caecilius nōn est in vīllā. Caecilius in forō negōtium agit.
Caecilius est argentārius. argentārius pecūniam numerat.
   Caecilius forum circumspectat. ecce! artifex in forō
ambulat. artifex est Clāra. Clāra Caecilium salūtat.
   ecce! tōnsor quoque est in forō. tōnsor est Pantagathus.
Caecilius tōnsōrem videt.
    'salvē!' Caecilius tōnsōrem salūtat.
    'salvē!' Pantagathus respondet.
    ecce! vēnālīcius forum intrat. vēnālīcius est Syphāx.
vēnālīcius mercātōrem exspectat. mercātor nōn venit.
Syphāx est īrātus. Syphāx mercātōrem vituperat.

negōtium agit
   is doing business
ecce! *look!*
artifex *artist*
5 **ambulat** *is walking*
tōnsor *barber*

vēnālīcius *slave dealer*
10 **nōn venit** *does not come*

artifex

artifex ad vīllam ambulat. artifex est Clāra. Clāra iānuam
pulsat. Clēmēns artificem nōn audit. servus est in hortō.
Clāra clāmat. canis Clāram audit et lātrat. Quīntus canem
audit. Quīntus ad iānuam venit. fīlius iānuam aperit. Clāra
Quīntum salūtat et vīllam intrat.

Metella est in culīnā. Quīntus mātrem vocat. Metella
ātrium intrat. artifex Metellam salūtat. Metella artificem ad
trīclīnium dūcit.

Clāra in trīclīniō labōrat. Clāra pictūram pingit. magnus
leō est in pictūrā. Herculēs quoque est in pictūrā. leō
Herculem ferōciter petit. Herculēs magnum fūstem tenet et
leōnem verberat. Herculēs est fortis.

Caecilius ad vīllam revenit et trīclīnium intrat. Caecilius
fīliam vocat. fīlia ad trīclīnium venit. Lūcia pictūram intentē
spectat et artificem laudat.

ad vīllam
*to the house, towards the
house*
iānuam pulsat
5   *knocks at the door*
aperit *opens*

dūcit *leads, takes*
pictūram pingit
10 *paints a picture*
magnus leō *big lion*
ferōciter *fiercely*
petit *is attacking*
fūstem tenet
15 *is holding a club*
verberat *is striking*
fortis *brave, strong*
revenit *returns*
intentē *closely, carefully*

Popular subjects for wall paintings in Roman houses include scenes from mythology, gardens and animals, and portraits: a scene from Greek mythology showing Iphigenia the daughter of the Greek king Agamemnon, found on the wall in Caecilius' tablinum (above, left); cupids playing hide and seek from the House of the Deer in Herculaneum (above, right); a cubiculum in the House of the Orchard in Pompeii covered in garden scenes with birds, plants, statues, fountains and decorative plaques displaying Egyptian motifs (right).

tōnsor

When you have read this story, answer the questions at the end. Answer in English unless you are asked for Latin.

tōnsor in tabernā labōrat. tōnsor est Pantagathus. Caecilius intrat.

    'salvē, tōnsor!' inquit Caecilius.

    'salvē!' respondet Pantagathus.

    tōnsor est occupātus. senex in sellā sedet. Pantagathus novāculam tenet et barbam tondet. senex novāculam intentē spectat.

    poēta tabernam intrat. poēta in tabernā stat et versum recitat. versus est scurrīlis. Caecilius rīdet. sed tōnsor nōn rīdet. tōnsor est īrātus.

    'furcifer! furcifer!' clāmat Pantagathus. senex est perterritus.

    tōnsor barbam nōn tondet. tōnsor senem secat. multus sanguis fluit.

    Caecilius surgit et ē tabernā exit.

in tabernā	*in the shop*
inquit	*says*
5 **occupātus**	*busy*
senex	*old man*
in sellā	*in the chair*
novāculam	*razor*
barbam tondet	
10	*is trimming his beard*
poēta	*poet*
versum recitat	
	recites a line, recites a verse
15 **scurrīlis**	*rude*
rīdet	*laughs, smiles*
sed	*but*
perterritus	*terrified*
secat	*cuts*
multus sanguis	*much blood*
fluit	*flows*
ē tabernā	*out of the shop*

Questions

1 **tōnsor in tabernā labōrat. tōnsor est Pantagathus. Caecilius intrat** (lines 1–2): who is the barber working in the shop when Caecilius enters?

2 **tōnsor est occupātus. senex in sellā sedet. Pantagathus novāculam tenet et barbam tondet** (lines 5–6): what is the barber busy trimming with a razor?

3 **poēta tabernam intrat. poēta in tabernā stat et versum recitat** (lines 8–9): who enters the shop to recite a verse?

4 **versus est scurrīlis. Caecilius rīdet** (line 9): what makes Caecilius laugh at the poet's verse?

5 **sed tōnsor nōn rīdet. tōnsor est īrātus** (lines 9–10): in what two ways does the barber react to the verse?

6 **tōnsor barbam nōn tondet. tōnsor senem secat** (line 13): what does the barber then do to the old man?

7 **Caecilius surgit et ē tabernā exit** (line 15): in what two ways does Caecilius react?

8 Look at the drawing of the barber and his customer. Find one Latin word in the story to describe the way the old man watches the razor.

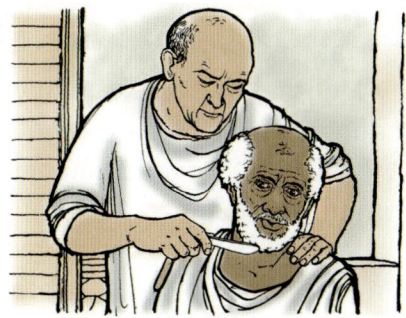

A pair of scissors.

ōrnātrīx

ancilla portum circumspectat. ancilla est Melissa. Melissa
prope nāvem stat. Melissa est anxia.

    Caecilius ad portum venit. Caecilius portum circumspectat.
argentārius Syphācem videt. Syphāx est vēnālīcius.

    'salvē, Syphāx!' clāmat argentārius. Syphāx Caecilium
salūtat et rīdet. Caecilius ancillam quaerit. vēnālīcius
Caecilium ad nāvem dūcit.

    'vīnum!' clāmat Syphāx. Melissa vīnum ad Caecilium
portat. argentārius vīnum bibit et Melissam spectat.

    'Melissa est docta,' inquit vēnālīcius. 'Melissa linguam
Latīnam discit. Melissa cēnam optimam coquit.'

    'sed Metella coquum habet,' inquit argentārius. 'Metella
ōrnātrīcem cupit.'

    'Melissa est ōrnātrīx optima,' inquit Syphāx. 'Melissa
crīnem compōnit. Melissa stolam compōnit. Melissa ...'

    'satis! satis!' clāmat Caecilius. Caecilius Melissam emit et ad
vīllam revenit. Caecilius Metellam vocat. Metella ancillam
intentē spectat et Caecilium laudat.

    Melissa vīllam circumspectat. Melissa est anxia.

Shackles with padlock.

ōrnātrīx *hairdresser, stylist*

portum *harbour*
prope nāvem *near a ship*
anxia *worried*

5

quaerit *is looking for*

10   **docta** *skilful*
linguam Latīnam discit
    is learning the Latin language
habet *has*
cupit *wants*
15   **crīnem compōnit** *arranges hair*
stolam *dress*
satis! *enough!*
emit *buys*

About the language

1   Remember the difference between the nominative case and accusative case of the following nouns:

nominative	Metella	Caecilius	mercātor
accusative	Metellam	Caecilium	mercātōrem

nominative case and **accusative case**: page 25

2   A large number of words, such as **fīlia** and **taberna**, form their accusative case in the same way as **Metella**. They are known as the **first declension** and look like this:

nominative	Metella	fīlia	taberna
accusative	Metellam	fīliam	tabernam

3   Another large group of nouns is known as the **second declension**. Most of these words form their accusative in the same way as **Caecilius**. For example:

nominative	Caecilius	amīcus	cibus
accusative	Caecilium	amīcum	cibum

4   You have also met several nouns belonging to the **third declension**. For example:

nominative	mercātor	leō	senex
accusative	mercātōrem	leōnem	senem

The nominative ending of the third declension may take various forms, but the accusative nearly always ends in **-em**.

Pompeian householders loved to have their walls painted with pictures of gardens full of flowers and birds, like this golden oriole.

Practising the language

in hortō

Grumio interrupts a story about Hercules.

Lūcia est in hortō. Lūcia fābulam recitat.

  Metella in hortō sedet et fīliam audit. Melissa in hortō labōrat. Melissa quoque Lūciam audit. Cerberus hortum intrat et circumspectat. ecce! canis ad culīnam ambulat.

  'Herculēs ad Orcum venit,' inquit Lūcia. 'magnus canis iānuam in Orcō custōdit. Herculēs magnum canem capit. canis ferōciter lātrat.'

  subitō Grumiō hortum intrat. Grumiō Cerberum ē culīnā dūcit. canis lātrat. coquus nōn est laetus.

  Lūcia Grumiōnem spectat. 'Herculēs est in hortō!' clāmat Lūcia. Metella fīliam laudat. Melissa rīdet.

fābulam story

5   **Orcum** *the underworld*
  custōdit *is guarding*
  capit *catches, captures*

10

---

1 **Explore the story**

  a **Lūcia est in hortō. Lūcia fābulam recitat** (line 1): where is Lucia and what is she doing?

  b **Melissa in hortō labōrat. Melissa quoque Lūciam audit** (lines 2–3): what two things is Melissa doing in the garden?

  c **Cerberus hortum intrat et circumspectat. ecce! canis ad culīnam ambulat** (lines 3–4): what two things does Cerberus do after he enters the garden?

  d **'magnus canis iānuam in Orcō custōdit. Herculēs magnum canem capit'** (lines 5–7): which one of the following statements is true?

    A A guard dog in the underworld catches Hercules.

    B Hercules catches a guard dog in the underworld.

  e **Grumiō Cerberum ē culīnā dūcit** (lines 8–9): where is Grumio leading Cerberus from?

  f **coquus nōn est laetus** (line 9): how does Grumio feel?

  g **'Herculēs est in hortō!' clāmat Lūcia** (lines 10–11): what does Lucia shout?

2 **Explore the language**

  a Find one Latin word from the story that is in the accusative case.

  b Now identify the declension of your word.

  c Find two more accusatives from the story, one from each of the two remaining declensions.

> **accusative case:** page 25
> **declension:** page 41

3 Explore further

Think about the whole story and then re-read lines 10–11 ('**Herculēs est in hortō!**'
clāmat Lūcia. Metella fīliam laudat).

Why do you think Metella praises Lucia at the end of the story?

Reviewing the language Stage 3: page 224

Enquiry: What would it be like to walk around Pompeii in AD 79?

The town of Pompeii

I knew nothing about Pompeii before I arrived here on Syphax's ship, and I was very worried about what kind of place it might be. The first thing I noticed was how incredibly busy the harbour was. There seemed to be merchants and ships from all over the world. I asked another of the enslaved women if she knew anything about Pompeii; luckily, she had grown up nearby and was happy to tell me about it.

Pompeii is at the crossroads of main coastal trade routes and the inland route along the river to towns like Nuceria. The area, Campania, is very fertile with good weather, and there are a number of prosperous towns around here. Outside the towns, especially along the coast, there are lots of villas and farming estates owned by wealthy Romans who have come here to enjoy the climate and beautiful countryside. I was scared that I would end up on a farm where the work might be dreadfully hard, but it seems that I'll be staying here in the city. I hope my work won't be too difficult or dangerous.

Pompeii covered 66 hectares (a hectare is 10 000 m² or just a little bigger than a rugby pitch) or 163 acres and was surrounded by a wall. The wall had twelve towers and, it is believed, eight gates. Only seven of these are confirmed, however; the eighth ('Capua Gate') is assumed to exist, but is in an area that is yet to be excavated. Roads led out from these gates to the harbour and to the neighbouring towns of Herculaneum, Nola, Nuceria and Stabiae.

Thinking point 1: Why do you think the town was surrounded by a wall and towers?

Villas along the bay. Detail from fresco found in the House of M. Lucretius Fronto in Pompeii.

Two wide main streets, known nowadays as the Via dell'Abbondanza (Street of Abundance) and Via Stabiana (Stabiae Street), crossed near the centre of the town. A third ran parallel to the Via dell'Abbondanza. These names are modern inventions to make it easier to identify the streets; we don't know what, if anything, the Pompeians called them. Sometimes people used local landmarks to help with directions; for example, the delivery address on a wine jar found at Pompeii reads 'To Euxinus, the innkeeper, at Pompeii, near the Amphitheatre'.

It's going to take me a while to find my way around Pompeii; I'm very scared of getting lost; I am going to have to ask for directions a lot.

The streets have high pavements on one or both sides of the road so you can avoid the traffic of wagons, horses and mules when you are walking. It also means you keep clear of the rubbish, dung, rainwater and the overflow from the fountains in the roadway. When you need to cross the road, you can use the stepping-stones to avoid getting your feet wet or dirty.

Thinking point 2: Look at this picture of a Pompeian street. Describe what you can see. What do historians claim was the purpose of the raised pieces of stone? What do you think made the ruts you can see running between them?

A street in Pompeii.

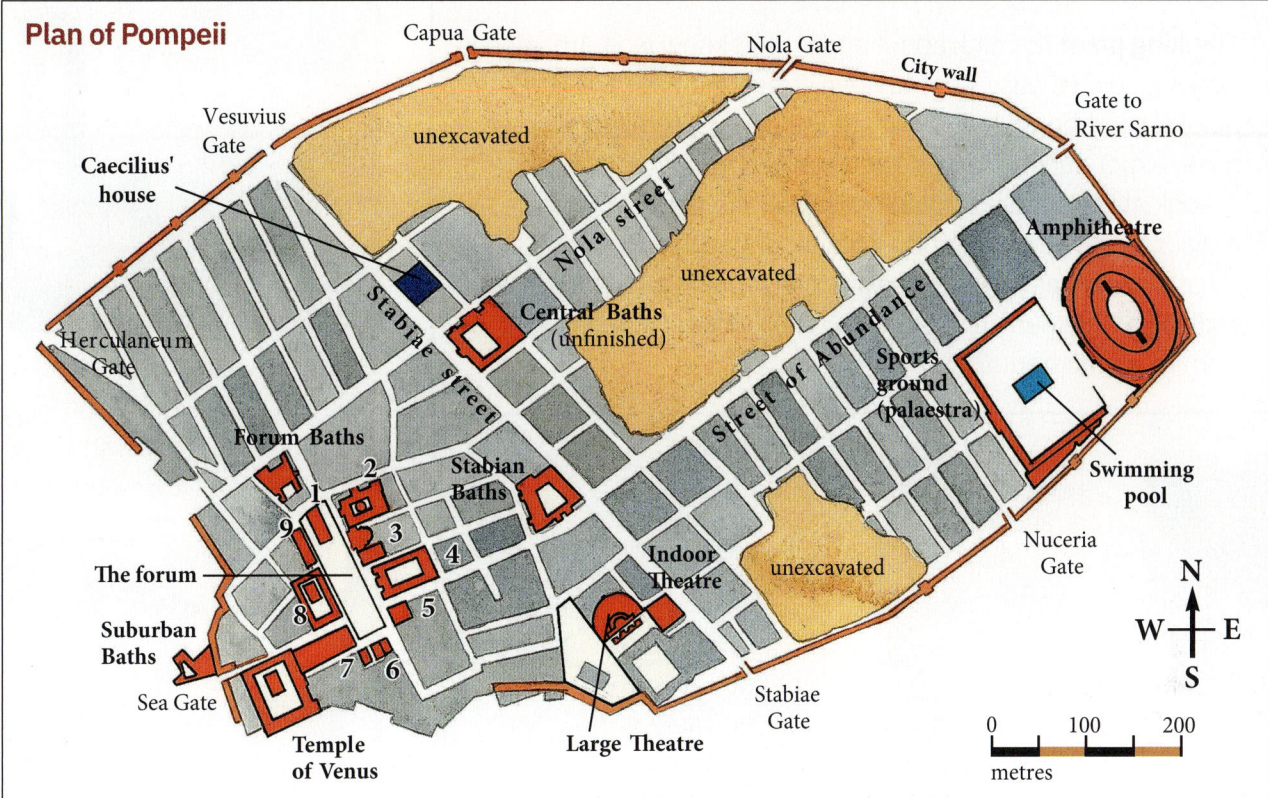

Plan of Pompeii

The buildings around the forum are usually identified as follows: 1 Temple of Jupiter; 2 Market; 3 Temples of the Emperors and the Lares of Pompeii; 4 Eumachia's building; 5 Open hall; 6 Possible government offices; 7 Basilica; 8 Temple of Apollo; 9 Vegetable market and public lavatory. More details on the buildings and their excavation can be found in Stage 4.

The town's water supply was brought by an aqueduct from a spring 42 kilometres (26 miles) away. It was distributed via lead pipes which ran beneath the pavements to 14 water towers usually built near crossroads, such as the one in the picture. Water was forced up into lead tanks on these towers by the pressure in the pipes. Public fountains, like the one next to the water tower in the picture, stood at many street corners and provided water to the businesses and households around them. Wealthier citizens paid special rates to get a private water supply straight into their homes.

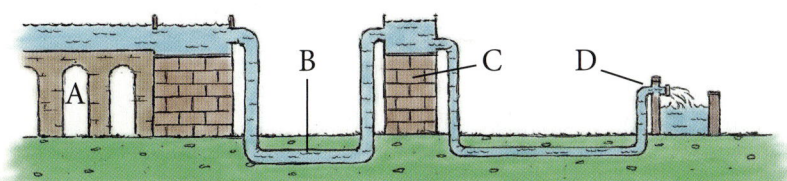

A: aqueduct; B: pipes; C: water tower; D: fountain.

Thinking point 3:
Caecilius has a delivery arriving on a ship. Find the Sea Gate (that leads to the harbour) on the map. Write out directions to lead the men making the delivery to Caecilius' house. Remember, there may not have been street names, so you need to use landmarks to help them find their way.

Crossroads of two main streets – Via dell' Abbondanza and Via Stabiana – with shops, stepping stones, fountain and water tower.

Counter with embedded storage jars (dolia), probably for dry goods such as nuts and dried fruits, and wine storage jars (amphorae) in the background.

Some bars also have wall paintings which show the customers drinking and gambling.

Narrower street lined with houses. One has a second storey overhanging the path to gain some extra space.

Apparently, the main shopping areas in Pompeii are in the forum and along the street leading to the river-gate. I expect I'll go there with and for Metella a lot; I'll have to carry anything she buys and run errands for her.

Carved or painted signs outside the shops and businesses sometimes tell you what they sell and do. I saw one depicting metal workers outside a place I think was a copper or bronze smith. All the main streets also have bakers' shops and bars where you can buy hot and cold drinks and snacks.

Plaque often interpreted as a shop sign, although its original location and purpose have been lost.

The forum in Pompeii contained several important religious buildings, but there were many others elsewhere in the town, including the Temple of Venus located near the gate to the harbour. The Pompeians had their own unique version of Venus – Venus Pompeiana – who was their patron deity. Each neighbourhood also had its own shrines in the streets and each home had its lararium. In this way, religion went from the State to the street to the home.

Another shop from Pompeii with a flour or grain mill, which would have been driven by enslaved people or donkeys, and a large, brick oven.

Thinking point 6: Look at the two pictures above. What sort of work may have happened in these buildings? How sure can you be about your claims? Which source is more useful?

Painting of Venus Pompeiana riding in a ship drawn by elephants from the facade of the House of Verecundus on the main street in Pompeii.

The whitewashed walls outside shops and houses have lots of advertisements and public notices painted on them. My Latin isn't good, but I can understand some of them. I've seen political slogans supporting candidates in the local elections, and adverts for gladiator fights and wild-animal hunts in the amphitheatre at the eastern end of town.

Pompeii is full of so many different types of people! You hear many different languages as you're walking around the town, and there are lots of different cultural influences. As well as people from all over Italy and my fellow Greeks, I've met and seen people from all over the Roman Empire including those from Syria, Africa and Spain.

A section of wall covered with painted slogans.

Pompeii would have been a thriving, multicultural society. We can see this diversity in the names found in the graffiti, in election campaign notices, in inscriptions on tombs, and even in Caecilius' own records. Among these are some names that might be Jewish; further evidence of this community includes fish sauce labelled as kosher and one inscription in Hebrew.

The Roman Empire in this period stretched from Britain in the northwest to Syria and Palestine in the east. The empire was held secure by soldiers stationed at strategic points, and troublemakers were not tolerated. Resistance or rebellion was handled without mercy.

Thinking point 7:
Think about your community; would a future historian be able to use similar methods to find out about its diversity? How easy or difficult do you think it would be?

Pompeii was well positioned for sea-trading and had excellent connections with the wider empire. The network of well-built roads created by the Romans made travel by land relatively easy, but for many purposes, particularly for trade, travel by sea was more convenient. Ships carried cargoes of building materials, foodstuffs and luxury goods across the Mediterranean and beyond. Some delicacies, such as pepper, made it as far as the frontier zone in Britain. As we see in this Stage, ships like Syphax's also carried cargoes of enslaved people like Melissa who might be transported far from home and sold into totally unfamiliar environments where they might not even speak the local language.

Relief from the tomb of freedwoman Naevoleia Tyche, showing a merchant ship and its crew.

Enquiry: What would it be like to walk around Pompeii in AD 79?

You may wish to consider the following:

- the sights, smells, and sounds you would experience
- the route you might be walking (use the map shown earlier in the Stage)
- the buildings you may pass
- the kind of streets you are on and the features they may have
- who and what else might be in the street
- what you may see on the walls of the buildings.

Vocabulary checklist 3

ad	to, towards	**nāvis**	ship
bibit	drinks	**nōn**	not
circumspectat	looks round	**portat**	carries
clāmat	shouts	**respondet**	replies
et	and	**rīdet**	laughs, smiles
exit	goes out	**salvē!**	hello!
exspectat	waits for	**sedet**	sits
iānua	door	**taberna**	shop
īrātus	angry	**videt**	sees
magnus	big	**vīnum**	wine

This painting shows Mercury, the god of profit as well as the messenger of the gods. Images of Mercury can be found all over Pompeii; this one was painted above a cloth workshop in the Street of Abundance, to bring success to the business.

1 Grumiō: ego sum coquus.
ego cēnam coquō.

2 Caecilius: ego sum argentārius.
ego pecūniam habeō.

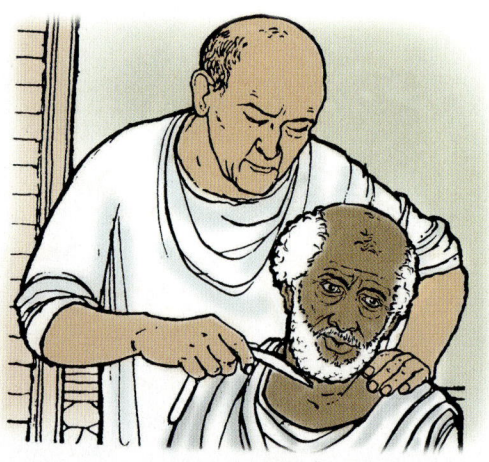

3 Pantagathus: ego sum tōnsor.
ego barbam tondeō.

4 Barbillus: ego sum mercātor.
ego vīnum vēndō.

5 poēta: ego sum poēta.
ego versum recitō.

6 Clāra: ego sum artifex.
ego leōnem pingō.

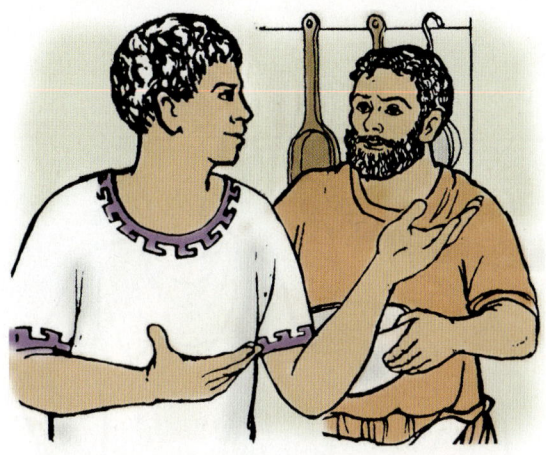

7 Quīntus: quid tū coquis?
   Grumiō: ego cēnam coquō.

8 Lūcia: quid tū habēs?
   Caecilius: ego pecūniam habeō.

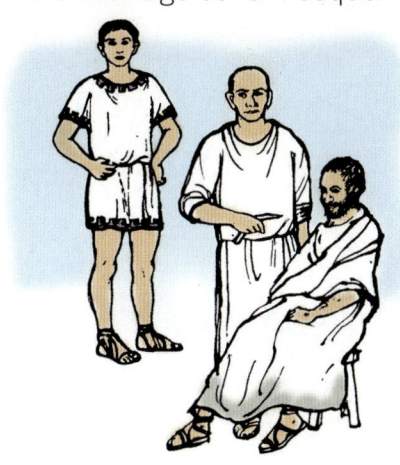

9 Quīntus: quid tū tondēs?
   tōnsor: ego barbam tondeō.

10 Lūcia: quid tū vēndis?
   mercātor: ego vīnum vēndō.

11 Quīntus: quid tū recitās?
   poēta: ego versum recitō.

12 Lūcia: quid tū pingis?
   artifex: ego leōnem pingō.

13 Metella: quis es tū?
    ancilla: ego sum Melissa.

14 Metella: quis es tu?
    artifex: ego sum Clāra.

15 Metella: quis es tū?
    tōnsor: ego sum Pantagathus.

A corner of the forum, with shops opening off a colonnade.

Hermogenēs

Caecilius est in forō. Caecilius in forō argentāriam habet.
Hermogenēs ad forum venit. Hermogenēs est mercātor
Graecus. mercātor nāvem habet. mercātor Caecilium
salūtat.

'ego sum mercātor Graecus,' inquit Hermogenēs. 'ego   5
sum mercātor probus. ego pecūniam quaerō.'

'cūr tū pecūniam quaeris?' inquit Caecilius. 'tū nāvem
habēs.'

'sed nāvis nōn adest,' respondet Hermogenēs. 'nāvis
est in Graeciā. ego pecūniam nōn habeō. ego tamen sum   10
probus. ego semper pecūniam reddō.'

'ecce!' inquit Caecilius. 'ego cēram habeō. tū ānulum
habēs?'

'ego ānulum habeō,' respondet Hermogenēs. 'ānulus
signum habet. ecce! ego signum in cērā imprimō.'   15

Caecilius pecūniam trādit. mercātor pecūniam capit et
ē forō currit.

ēheu! Hermogenēs nōn revenit. mercātor pecūniam
nōn reddit.

Caecilius Hermogenem ad basilicam vocat.   20

argentāriam	*banker's stall*
Graecus	*Greek*
probus	*honest*
cūr?	*why?*
nōn adest	*is not here*
in Graeciā	*in Greece*
tamen	*however*
semper	*always*
ego reddō	*I give back*
cēram	*wax tablet*
ānulum	*ring*
signum	*seal*
ego imprimō	*I press*
trādit	*hands over*
capit	*takes*
currit	*runs*
basilicam	*law court*

About the language 1

1   In the first three Stages, you met sentences like this:

fīlia ambulat.   mercātor sedet.   amīcus currit.
The daughter walks.   *The merchant sits.*   *The friend runs.*

All of these sentences have a noun (**fīlia**, **mercātor**, **amīcus**) and a word indicating the action of the sentence, known as the **verb**. In the sentences above the verbs are **ambulat**, **sedet**, **currit**.

In all the sentences you met in the first three Stages, the verb ended in **-t**.

2   In Stage 4, you have met sentences with **ego** and **tū**:

ego ambulō.   *I walk.*   **ego** sedeō.   *I sit.*   **ego** currō.   *I run.*
tū ambulās.   *You walk.*   **tū** sedēs.   *You sit.*   **tū** curris.   *You run.*

3   Notice the three different forms of each verb:

ego ambul**ō**.   ego sede**ō**.   ego curr**ō**.
tū ambulā**s**.   tū sedē**s**.   tū curri**s**.
fīlia ambula**t**.   mercātor sede**t**.   amīcus curri**t**.

Notice also that the words **ego** and **tū** are not strictly necessary, since the endings **-ō** and **-s** make it clear that 'I' and 'you' are performing the action of the sentence. The Romans generally used **ego** and **tū** for emphasis.

4   The following example is rather different:

ego **sum** īrātus.   tū **es** īrātus.   amīcus **est** īrātus.
I am angry.   *You are angry.*   *The friend is angry.*

5   Further examples:

   a   Lūcia recitat. ego recitō.

   b   Quīntus dormit. tū dormīs.

   c   tū labōrās. amīcus labōrat.

   d   mercātor vīnum habet. ego vīnum habeō.

   e   ego pecūniam trādō. tū pecūniam trādis.

   f   Pantagathus est tōnsor. tū es mercātor. ego sum poēta.

   g   ambulō. circumspectō. circumspectās. es.

   h   sum. audiō. audīs. habēs.

in basilicā

iūdex basilicam intrat.

iūdex:	quis es tū?
Caecilius:	ego sum Lūcius Caecilius Iūcundus.
iūdex:	tū es Pompēiānus?
Caecilius:	ego sum Pompēiānus.
iūdex:	quid tū in urbe agis?
Caecilius:	ego cotīdiē ad forum veniō. ego sum argentārius.
iūdex:	cūr tū hodiē ad basilicam venīs?
Caecilius:	Hermogenēs multam pecūniam dēbet. Hermogenēs pecūniam nōn reddit.
Hermogenēs:	Caecilius est mendāx!
iūdex:	quis es tū?
Hermogenēs:	ego sum Hermogenēs.
iūdex:	Hermogenēs, quid tū in urbe agis?
Hermogenēs:	ego in forō negōtium agō. ego sum mercātor.
iūdex:	quid tū respondēs? tū pecūniam dēbēs?
Hermogenēs:	ego pecūniam nōn dēbeō. amīcus meus est testis.
amīcus:	ego sum testis. Hermogenēs pecūniam nōn dēbet. Caecilius est mendāx.
Caecilius:	tū, Hermogenēs, es mendāx. amīcus tuus quoque est mendāx. tū pecūniam nōn reddis ...
iūdex:	satis! tū Hermogenem accūsās, sed tū rem nōn probās.
Caecilius:	ego cēram habeō. tū signum in cērā vidēs.
Hermogenēs:	ēheu!
iūdex:	Hermogenēs, tū ānulum habēs?
Caecilius:	ecce! Hermogenēs ānulum cēlat.
iūdex:	ubi est ānulus? ecce! ānulus rem probat. ego Hermogenem convincō.

5

10

15

20

25

iūdex *judge*
quis? *who?*

Pompēiānus *Pompeian*

quid tū agis? *what do you do?*
in urbe *in the city*
cotīdiē *every day*
hodiē *today*
dēbet *owes*

mendāx *liar*

meus *my*
testis *witness*

tuus *your*

tū accūsās *you accuse*
tū rem nōn probās
  you do not prove the case

cēlat *is hiding*
ubi? *where*
ego convincō
  I convict, I find guilty

Some sealstones from rings and the face of a gold seal ring without a stone.

About the language 2

1   In this Stage, you have met the following ways of asking questions in Latin:

By tone of voice, indicated in writing just by a question mark:

tū ānulum habēs?	*Do you have the ring?*
tū es Pompēiānus?	*Are you a Pompeian?*

By means of a question word such as **cūr**, **quis**, **quid** or **ubi**:

cūr tū pecūniam quaeris?	*Why are you looking for money?*
quis es tū?	*Who are you?*
quid tū in urbe agis?	*What do you do in the city?*
ubi est ānulus?	*Where is the ring?*

2   Further examples:

a   cūr tū in hortō labōrās?

b   quis est artifex?

c   tū pecūniam habēs?

d   ubi est mercātor?

e   quid tū quaeris, Melissa?

f   quis vīnum portat?

g   tū cēnam parās?

h   ubi es tū?

The basilica (law court) was a large, long building with rows of pillars inside and a high platform at the far end on which the town's senior officials may have sat when hearing lawsuits.

Practising the language

Grumiō et leō

Not everyone pictures Grumio as Hercules.

Melissa in trīclīniō stat. Melissa Herculem in pictūrā spectat.
ancilla rīdet et Grumiōnem vocat. Grumiō trīclīnium intrat.
  'ecce!' inquit Melissa. 'tū es in pictūrā! magnus leō tē
ferōciter petit. sed tū es fortis. tū leōnem verberās.'
  Clēmēns trīclīnium intrat.   5
  'ecce!' inquit coquus. 'quis est in pictūrā?'
  Clēmēns nōn respondet.
  'tū linguam habēs?' inquit Grumiō. 'ego sum in pictūrā!
leō mē petit. ego fūstem teneō et leōnem verberō.'
  'quid tū dīcis?' respondet Clēmēns. 'tū es in pictūrā?   10
tū es coquus magnificus, Grumiō. sed ego tē in pictūrā
nōn videō.'

linguam *tongue*
quid tū dīcis?
    what are you saying?
magnificus
    impressive, magnificent

1 **Explore the story**

   a **Melissa Herculem in pictūrā spectat. ancilla rīdet et Grumiōnem vocat** (lines 1–2):
      which two of the following statements are true?

      A Melissa is looking at a picture of Hercules.

      B Hercules is looking at a picture of Melissa.

      C Grumio calls Melissa and smiles.

      D Melissa smiles and calls Grumio.

   b **'ecce!' inquit Melissa. 'tū es in pictūrā!'** (line 3): what does Melissa tell Grumio?

   c **'sed tū es fortis. tū leōnem verberās'** (line 4): what two things does Melissa say
      about Grumio?

   d **'ecce!' inquit coquus. 'quis est in pictūrā?'**

      Clēmēns nōn respondet.

      'tū linguam habēs?' inquit Grumiō (line 6–8): what two questions does Grumio ask
      Clemens?

   e **'quid tū dīcis?' respondet Clēmēns. 'tū es in pictūrā?** (line 10): what does Clemens
      say in reply to Grumio?

   f **tū es coquus magnificus, Grumiō'** (line 11): write down the Latin word that tell us
      what Clemens thinks of Grumio. Which of the two possible translations of this word
      do you think is best here?

2 Explore the language

Explain why **verberās** (line 4) and
verberō (line 9) have different endings.

verb endings: page 56

3 Explore further

Think about the whole story and reread line 8 (**'ego sum in pictūrā!'**).

Do you think that Grumio is being serious when he says this?

Reviewing the language Stage 4: page 225

An artist's impression of a Roman-style trial. The judge and his advisers
are sitting up on the platform listening to the arguments being made by
one of the advocates. The accused man stands nearby and
there are soldiers on hand to keep order.

**Enquiry: The word 'forum' is often translated as 'marketplace'.
To what extent do you think this is a good translation?**

The forum

The forum was the heart of business, religion and local
government in Pompeii. It was a large open space 143 metres
long and 38 metres wide (156 yards and 42 yards) paved
with stone and surrounded on three sides by a colonnade
with columns of white marble. Various important buildings
stood around it and it contained a number of statues
commemorating the emperor, members of his family and local
citizens who had given distinguished service to the town.

Part of the colonnade, which had two storeys, seen from inside. You can see the holes for the floor beams of the top storey.

A very rich local woman named Julia Felix asked me to decorate her atrium with wall paintings of typical scenes in the forum. I based some on the sights you might see on market day. In the following picture, the trader on the left has set up his wooden stall and is selling small articles of ironware including pincers, knives and hammers; the trader on the right is a shoemaker. He has seated his customers on stools while he shows them his goods. Behind the traders is the colonnade, which provides an open corridor in which people can walk and do business sheltered from the summer sun or winter rain.

In the back of the picture are two statues of important citizens mounted on horseback. Between them is one of the bronze gates through which people enter the forum. The whole forum area is only for pedestrians, mules and horses; a row of upright stones at each entrance blocks wheeled traffic like wagons.

Drawing based on Pompeian wall paintings from the House of Julia Felix. The original paintings are badly damaged, but this recreates several details from them.

> **Thinking point 1:** Think back to Stage 1: what subjects did most people choose for the wall paintings in their houses? What does Julia Felix's choice suggest about her?

The largest building near the forum may have been a market; perhaps for cloth, other products, or even, it has recently been argued, enslaved people. An inscription tells us that a Pompeian woman named Eumachia paid for it to be built. Eumachia inherited money from her father and was a priestess and a patron of the clothworkers. The inscription reads:

A painting from Julia Felix's atrium. This one is well preserved enough for us to make out the noticeboards, the people reading them and the statues behind the boards.

This statue of a distinguished citizen on horseback was found in nearby Herculaneum, but is very similar to the left-hand statue in the painting from Julia Felix's atrium.

Statue of Eumachia. The inscription reads: 'To Eumachia, daughter of Lucius, public priestess; the clothworkers set this up.'

In another of my wall paintings from Julia Felix's house, you can see people studying the public noticeboards fixed across the pedestals of three statues. If you want to know the election results or dates of processions and shows, you will find them on these boards.

In addition to official announcements, the forum – in fact the whole of Pompeii – is covered in graffiti. People put up notices about lost property, advertise accommodation to let (Julia Felix advertises her rooms to rent like this, actually), leave messages to lovers and publicise the problems they are having with their neighbours. Some of the things people write are incredibly rude!

Thinking point 2: Are there modern equivalents for the forum noticeboards and Pompeian graffiti?

People wrote graffiti for a wide variety of reasons, for example:

> **'A bronze jar has been lost from this shop. A reward is offered for its recovery.'**

> **'Macerior requests that the aedile [*the official who was responsible for law and order*] stop people from making a noise in the streets and disturbing decent folk who are asleep.'**

One of the longest and most elaborate pieces of graffiti is a seven-line poem found scratched into the wall of a hallway of a house in Pompeii. The opening lines read:

> **'Oh, if only I could have your little arms wrapped around my neck and press kisses to your delicate little lips. Come now, my little darling, trust your happiness to the winds.'**

This piece is remarkable not only for its length and complexity, but also because the form of the Latin suggests that this may be the only known Latin love poem from one woman to another.

Some of the most important public buildings were situated around the forum. It can sometimes be hard to interpret the uses of buildings from what remains. People probably removed things as they fled the city, and some buildings were tunnelled into and looted before they could be studied. Certain finds can be very helpful to historians and archaeologists, though, and comparisons with other towns can also suggest the use of a building.

> **Thinking point 3:** Think about a modern building you know well. Do you think future archaeologists might find it difficult to interpret what it was used for? What clues might they have?

The Temple of the Capitoline Triad: Jupiter, Juno and Minerva.

The buildings of the forum

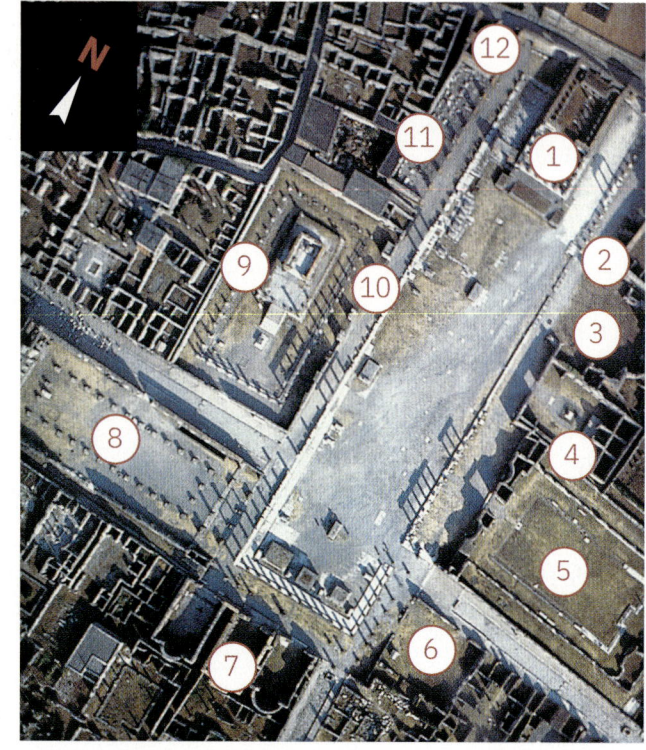

1 Temple of Jupiter, Juno and Minerva
2 Market
3 Temple of the Lares
4 Temple of the Emperors
5 Eumachia's building
6 Open hall, possibly used for voting and auctions
7 Possible government offices
8 Basilica
9 Temple of Apollo
10 Weights and measures table
11 Vegetable market
12 Toilets

On the east side of the forum is the large building built with money given by Eumachia (5). Next to it was an open hall (6) which may have been used for voting in elections, but the raised platforms found in the hall suggest it could also have been a venue for auctions, including those of enslaved people.

Along the south side were three buildings (7) which may have been local government offices, perhaps a treasury, record office or council chamber. There is, however, very little evidence for this. An alternative theory, based on similar buildings in other Roman Italian towns, is that they were built by wealthy families to honour their ancestors or the emperor. At the southwest corner stood the basilica, or law court (8), which was also used as a meeting place for businessmen. At one end of this building is a raised platform, possibly for auctions or trials.

Diagonally opposite the basilica is a large covered market (2) which contained permanent shops rather than temporary stalls. The remains of fish bones and scales were found here, suggesting this was a meat and fish market. Across from this was another building thought to be a market (11), although it may not have been in use when the city was destroyed (it was discovered with no roof and the walls were not plastered). It has been suggested that this market may have been for things like grain, as it is near the public weights and measures table (10). This table was where traders' measures were checked to make sure they were accurate and fair. Nearby is a set of public toilets (12).

In a prominent position at the north end stood a temple of Jupiter, Juno and Minerva (1) (see page 63). These three were known as the Capitoline Triad, the most important of the Roman gods, and temples to them were common throughout the empire. The temple had three chambers, one dedicated to each of the gods, and a huge marble head of Jupiter was found during excavations. Candidates in elections probably made speeches standing on the steps of this temple.

Immediately to the south of the meat and fish market is a temple traditionally thought to be dedicated to the Lares, the guardian spirits of Pompeii (3). Recent comparisons with other towns in Roman Italy, however, suggest it may actually have been a place to display statues of members of the imperial family. While there are places for housing statues in this temple, none survive to suggest which theory is correct.

Next to this is a rectangular building (4) thought to be a temple in honour of the Roman emperors: it has an altar decorated with imperial symbols, such as an oak wreath and laurels, and showing the sacrifice of a bull to the emperor. Across the forum from this was the Temple of Apollo (9).

Thinking point 4:
Give an example of a building in Pompeii's forum which has more than one suggested interpretation of its use and explain why this is.

Enquiry: The word 'forum' is often translated as 'marketplace'. To what extent do you think this is a good translation?

You may wish to consider the following:

- the forum's role in politics, trade and religion
- the types of building found in the forum
- evidence for different activities that went on in the forum
- modern equivalents to the forum.

Vocabulary checklist 4

agit	*does*
ānulus	*ring*
coquit	*cooks*
cūr?	*why?*
ē	*from, out of*
ecce!	*look!*
ego	*I*
ēheu!	*oh dear! oh no!*
forum	*forum, marketplace*
habet	*has*
inquit	*says*
pecūnia	*money*
perterritus	*terrified*
quaerit	*looks for, searches for*
quis?	*who?*
reddit	*gives back*
satis	*enough*
sed	*but*
tū	*you*
vocat	*calls*

This marble carving shows the Temple of the Capitoline Triad in the forum with statues of men on horseback on each side. This is a section from a larger piece depicting scenes in Pompeii during the earthquake of AD 62 or 63, which was found in Caecilius' house.

in viā

1 canis est in viā.

2 canēs sunt in viā.

3 amīcus est in viā.

4 amīcī sunt in viā.

5 puella est in viā.

6 puellae sunt in viā.

7 puer est in viā.

8 puerī sunt in viā.

9 mercātor est in viā.

10 mercātōrēs sunt in viā.

in theātrō

11 spectātor in theātrō sedet.

12 spectātōrēs in theātrō sedent.

13 āctor in scaenā stat.

14 āctōrēs in scaenā stant.

15 fēmina spectat.

16 fēminae spectant.

17 senex dormit.

18 senēs dormiunt.

19 iuvenis plaudit.

20 iuvenēs plaudunt.

āctōrēs

magna turba est in urbe. fēminae et puellae sunt in turbā.
senēs quoque et iuvenēs sunt in turbā. servī hodiē nōn
labōrant. senēs hodiē nōn dormiunt. mercātōrēs hodiē nōn
sunt occupātī. Pompēiānī sunt ōtiōsī.

urbs tamen nōn est quiēta. Pompēiānī ad theātrum
contendunt. magnus clāmor est in urbe.

agricolae urbem intrant. nautae urbem petunt. pāstōrēs
dē monte veniunt et ad urbem contendunt. turba per
portam ruit.

nūntius in forō clāmat: 'āctōrēs sunt in urbe. āctōrēs sunt
in theātrō. Priscus fābulam dat. Priscus fābulam optimam
dat. āctōrēs sunt Actius et Sorex.'

Caecilius et Metella ē vīllā discēdunt. argentārius et
uxor ad theātrum ambulant. Quīntus et Lūcia ad theātrum
contendunt. Clēmēns et Melissa ad theātrum currunt. sed
Grumiō in vīllā manet.

āctōrēs *actors*

turba *crowd*
fēminae *women*
puellae *girls*
sunt *are*
5 **iuvenēs** *young people*
ōtiōsī
    on holiday, taking time off
quiēta *quiet*
ad theātrum contendunt
10   *hurry to the theatre*
clāmor *noise, shouting*
agricolae *farmers*
nautae *sailors*
petunt *make for, head for*
15 **pāstōrēs** *shepherds*
dē monte
    down from the mountain
per portam ruit
    rushes through the gate
nūntius *messenger*
fābulam dat
    is putting on a play
discēdunt *depart, leave*
uxor *wife*
manet *remains, stays*

Terracotta statues of actors wearing masks
and costumes. Both would have been
male, although one is dressed as a woman.
They were found at the entrance to a
private garden near the theatres and were
originally brightly painted.

About the language 1

1   In the first four Stages, you have met sentences like these:

fīlia sedet.	amīcus labōrat.
The daughter is sitting.	*The friend is working.*
leō currit.	mercātor dormit.
The lion is running.	*The merchant is sleeping.*

Sentences like these refer to **one** person or thing, and in each sentence the form of both words (the noun and the verb) is said to be **singular**.

2   Sentences which refer to **more than one** person or thing use a different form of the words, known as the **plural**. Compare the singular and plural forms in the following sentences:

singular	*plural*
puella labōrat.	puellae labōrant.
The girl is working.	*The girls are working.*
amīcus rīdet.	amīcī rīdent.
The friend is laughing.	*The friends are laughing.*
leō currit.	leōnēs currunt.
The lion is running.	*The lions are running.*
mercātor dormit.	mercātōrēs dormiunt.
The merchant is sleeping.	*The merchants are sleeping.*

Note that in each of these sentences **both** the noun and the verb show the difference between singular and plural.

3   Look again at the sentences in paragraph 2 and note the difference between the singular and plural forms of the verb.

singular	*plural*
labōrat	labōrant
rīdet	rīdent
currit	currunt
dormit	dormiunt

For each verb the singular ending is **-t** and the plural ending is **-nt**.

4   Notice how Latin shows the difference between 'is' and 'are':

mercātor **est** in viā.	mercātōrēs **sunt** in viā.
The merchant is in the street.	*The merchants are in the street.*

Poppaea

Poppaea est ancilla. ancilla prope iānuam stat. ancilla viam spectat.
dominus in hortō dormit. dominus est Lucriō. Lucriō est senex.

Poppaea:	ego amīcum meum exspectō. ubi est amīcus?	
	(Lucriō stertit.)	
	ēheu! Lucriō est in vīllā.	5
	(agricolae in viā clāmant.)	
agricolae:	euge! agricolae hodiē nōn labōrant!	**euge!** *hurray!*
Poppaea:	Lucriō! Lucriō! agricolae urbem intrant. agricolae adsunt.	**adsunt** *are here*
Lucriō:	*(sēmisomnus)* a … a … agricolae?	10 **sēmisomnus** *half asleep*
puerī:	euge! Sorex! Actius! āctōrēs adsunt.	
Poppaea:	Lucriō! Lucriō! puerī per viam currunt.	**puerī** *boys*
Lucriō:	quid tū clāmās, Poppaea? cūr tū clāmōrem facis?	**per viam** *along the road*
Poppaea:	Lucriō, Pompēiānī clāmōrem faciunt.	**tū facis** *you are making*
	agricolae et puerī sunt in viā.	15
Lucriō:	cūr tū mē vexās?	**tū vexās** *you are annoying*
Poppaea:	āctōrēs in theātrō fābulam agunt.	
Lucriō:	āctōrēs?	
Poppaea:	Sorex et Actius adsunt.	
Lucriō:	quid tū dīcis?	20
Poppaea:	*(īrāta)* senēs ad theātrum ambulant, iuvenēs ad theātrum contendunt, omnēs Pompēiānī	**omnēs** *all*
	ad theātrum ruunt. āctōrēs in theātrō fābulam agunt.	**fābulam agunt** *are acting out a play*
Lucriō:	euge! āctōrēs adsunt. ego quoque ad theātrum contendō.	25
	(exit Lucriō.)	
Poppaea:	euge! Lucriō abest!	**abest** *is out*
	(amīcus vīllam intrat.)	
amīcus:	salvē! mea columba!	**mea columba** *my dove, darling*
Poppaea:	Grumiō, dēliciae meae! salvē!	30 **dēliciae meae** *my sweetheart*

About the language 2

1   Study the following examples of singular and plural forms:

singular	*plural*
puella rīdet.	**puellae** rīdent.
The girl is smiling.	*The girls are smiling.*
amīcus ambulat.	**amīcī** ambulant.
The friend is walking.	*The friends are walking.*
mercātor contendit.	**mercātōrēs** contendunt.
The merchant is hurrying.	*The merchants are hurrying.*

2   Each of the nouns in **bold** is in the nominative case, because it refers to a person or persons who are performing some action, such as walking or smiling.

3   **puella**, **amīcus** and **mercātor** are therefore **nominative singular**, and **puellae**, **amīcī** and **mercātōrēs** are **nominative plural**.

4   Notice the forms of the nominative plural in the different declensions:

first declension	*second declension*	*third declension*
puellae	amīcī	mercātōrēs
ancillae	fīliī	leōnēs
fēminae	puerī	senēs

5   Further examples:

   a   fīlius ambulat. fīliī ambulant.

   b   āctor clāmat. āctōrēs clāmant.

   c   fēminae plaudunt. fēmina plaudit.

   d   argentāriī intrant. argentārius intrat.

   e   fīlia respondet. fīliae respondent.

   f   senēs dormiunt. senex dormit.

6   Examples with **est** and **sunt:**

   a   spectātor est in theātrō. spectātōrēs sunt in theātrō.

   b   fēminae sunt in forō. fēmina est in forō.

   c   amīcī sunt in trīclīniō. amīcus est in trīclīniō.

   d   agricola adest. agricolae adsunt.

Practising the language

in theātrō

Exciting news interrupts the performance of a play.

hodiē Pompēiānī sunt ōtiōsī. multī Pompēiānī in
theātrō sedent. spectātōrēs clāmōrem nōn faciunt.
spectātōrēs Actium exspectant. euge! tandem Actius
in scaenā stat. Pompēiānī plaudunt.

    Actius in scaenā fābulam agit. fābula est scurrīlis.   5
iuvenēs rīdent et Actium laudant. senēs nōn dormiunt.
senēs quoque Actium laudant. sed puerī et puellae
sunt perterritī. Actius est persōnātus.

    subitō Pompēiānī magnum clāmōrem audiunt.
nūntius theātrum intrat. 'fūnambulus! fūnambulus   10
adest!' clāmat nūntius. 'fūnambulus est Prūdēns!'

    Pompēiānī Actium nōn spectant. omnēs Pompēiānī
ē theātrō currunt et Prūdentem spectant. nēmō in
theātrō manet.

    Actius tamen nōn est īrātus. Actius quoque   15
fūnambulum spectat.

multī *many*
spectātōrēs *spectators*
tandem *at last*
in scaenā *on the stage*
plaudunt *applaud, clap*

persōnātus
   wearing a mask
subitō *suddenly*
fūnambulus
   tightrope walker
nēmō *no one*

---

1 **Explore the story**

    a **euge! tandem Actius in scaenā stat. Pompēiānī plaudunt** (lines 3–4): why are the
        Pompeians applauding?

    b **Actius in scaenā fābulam agit. fābula est scurrīlis** (line 5): write down and translate
        the Latin word that describes the play Actius is performing in.

    c **iuvenēs rīdent et Actium laudant. senēs nōn dormiunt. senēs quoque Actium laudant**
        (lines 6–7): what do the young people and the old men both do to show they are
        enjoying the play?

    d **sed puerī et puellae sunt perterritī. Actius est persōnātus** (lines 7–8): what effect
        does Actius' mask have on the boys and girls?

    e Look at line 10 (**'fūnambulus!'**). Since the Latin verb **ambulat** means *walks* or *is
        walking*, what do you think the noun **fūnis** means?

f nēmō in theātrō manet. Actius tamen nōn est īrātus. Actius quoque fūnambulum **spectat** (lines 13–16): which three of the following statements are true?

   A Everyone stays in the theatre.   **D** Actius is angry.

   B No one stays in the theatre.   **E** Actius is watching the tightrope walker.

   C Actius is not angry.   **F** The tightrope walker is watching Actius.

2 Explore the language

Find two Latin verbs from the story that are plural.

plurals: page 73

3 Explore further

Think about the whole story and then reread **multī Pompēiānī in theātrō sedent** (lines 1–2). In this story, what different things do the Pompeians find entertaining at the theatre?

Reviewing the language Stage 5: page 226

Enquiry: How would attending the theatre in Pompeii have compared with modern experiences of theatrical performance?

The theatre at Pompeii

Thinking point 1: Choose three of your favourite TV shows or films. Imagine that in 2000 years the scripts of these have survived to be studied. What would future historians be able to learn about us? What wouldn't they be able to learn? What misconceptions might they form? What other evidence would be useful for them to consider alongside the scripts?

Plays are not performed in Pompeii every day, only several times a year at festivals, so it's exciting when notices appear announcing a performance! Performances are free to attend. All the costs are paid by a wealthy citizen, who provides the actors, the producer, the scenery and the costumes. They do this to benefit the rest of the people living in the town … but also to make themselves popular before standing in local political elections!

On the day of the performance the shops are closed and no business is done in the forum. Everyone sets off for the theatre early in the morning to try to get good seats. The town councillors and other important citizens don't need to hurry; the best seats at the front of the auditorium are reserved for them. Some people take cushions, because the seats are made of stone, and lots of people take food and drink for the day.

Thinking point 2: What does Clemens' description suggest about the role of the theatre in Roman society? To what extent is this different from modern theatre?

The large theatre at Pompeii could hold 5000 people, about half the population of the town. It seems that everyone could attend the theatre, although it's likely that enslaved people would have had to ask permission to go. It is uncertain whether men and women sat separately or together; women may have had to make do with a seat at the top of the large semicircular auditorium with a more distant view of the actors.

Pompeii's large theatre.

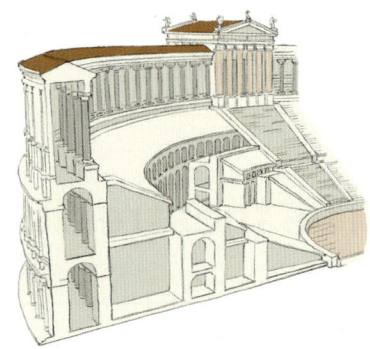

Seating in the theatre was arranged on an upwards slope away from the stage so that people further back could see over the heads of the people in front.

Thinking point 3: How does the shape of the theatre help the audience to enjoy the performance?

Performances consist of a series of plays which last all day. It can get really hot in the afternoon in Pompeii, so to keep the audience cool a large awning is suspended by ropes and pulleys across most of the theatre. This is managed by sailors, who are used to handling ropes and canvas. If it is a windy day, the awning can't be unfurled, and we have to use hats or sunshades to protect ourselves from the sun. Between plays, scented water is sprinkled by attendants.

One of the most popular kinds of production was the pantomime, a mixture of opera and ballet totally unlike modern pantomimes. The plot, which was usually serious, was taken from Greek myth. The parts of the different characters were mimed and danced by one masked performer while a chorus sang the lyrics. An orchestra containing instruments such as the lyre, double pipes, trumpet and castanets accompanied the performance, providing a rhythmical beat. Although there is evidence that women and girls sometimes performed in pantomimes, most performers were men, usually enslaved Greek men or freedmen. They were much admired for their skill and stamina and attracted a large following of fans.

Pantomime actors dressed like tragic actors in cloak and tunic and wore different masks to play different characters. The masks were very stylised with big, bold features.

Fragment of a wall painting showing an actor in the dressing room, studying his mask.

Equally popular were the comic actors. The bronze statue of one of these, Sorex, was discovered at Pompeii, together with graffiti on walls naming other popular actors. One of these reads:

'Actius, our favourite, come back quickly.'

Comic actors were always male and performed short plays which were often put on at the end of longer performances. These were about Italian country life and were full of rude jokes and slapstick. They used just a few familiar characters, such as Pappus, an easily fooled old man, and Maccus, a clown. These characters were instantly recognisable from the masks worn by the actors. These masks, like those used in other plays, were probably made of linen which was covered with plaster and painted.

A clay model of a mask.

Thinking point 4: Why do you think these comic plays were put on at the end of longer performances?

Thinking point 5: Why do you think actors wore masks with such bold features?

Sometimes, at a festival, the comedies of Plautus and Terence may have been put on. Plautus' comedies, which are among the earliest surviving literary texts in Latin, tend to be based on Greek scripts.

> I think my favourite plays are by Plautus and Terence. They are funny and use some familiar characters, but the plots are more complicated than the shorter comedies and the dialogue is a bit cleverer as well. In Plautus' comedies the enslaved characters also often mastermind the plot and outwit their enslavers, which I really enjoy.

The comedies of Plautus often have standard plotlines and make use of 'stock' characters such as the Old Man or Young Lover. These were easily recognisable for the audience because of their frequent use and stereotypical portrayal. There is usually a young man from a respectable family, who is leading a wild life, often in debt and in love with an enslaved woman. This all has to be kept from his father because he would disapprove. The son is usually helped by a clever enslaved man, who gets them into and out of trouble. Eventually it is discovered that the woman is not enslaved at all, but freeborn and from a well-respected family. The young man is therefore able to marry his true love and live happily ever after.

> **Thinking point 6:** Can you give any examples of popular modern films or TV shows that have 'stock characters' or predictable plots? Think about the kind of people these 'stock' figures tend to be. What are the problems with such stereotypes being used so often?

Scenes from a Plautine comedy

1 Father has to be restrained from violence when he finds his son coming home drunk from a party. The clever enslaved man props the lad up. A musician is playing the double pipes.

2 The boy has been with his beloved enslaved woman. This is the kind of mask the performer playing her may have worn.

3 The enslaved man sits on an altar for sanctuary, hoping to escape terrible punishment.

4 The enslaved man uncovers the woman's basket and finds her baby clothes which are immediately recognised; she must be the long-lost daughter of the father's best friend, who was stolen by pirates!

Enquiry: How would attending the theatre in Pompeii have compared with modern experiences of theatrical performance?

You may wish to consider the following:

- the theatre building itself and the nature of the audience.
- how the shows were funded and their role in Roman society
- the types of performances people might have watched
- the actors and how they went about their performance
- the most significant similarities and differences.

Vocabulary checklist 5

adest	*is here*	**multus**	*much*
adsunt	*are here*	**multī**	*many*
agricola	*farmer*	**optimus**	*excellent, best*
ambulat	*walks*	**petit**	*heads for, attacks*
audit	*hears, listens to*	**plaudit**	*applauds, claps*
clāmor	*noise, shouting*	**puella**	*girl*
contendit	*hurries*	**senex**	*old man*
currit	*runs*	**spectat**	*looks at, watches*
fābula	*play, story*	**stat**	*stands*
fēmina	*woman*	**turba**	*crowd*
hodiē	*today*	**ubi?**	*where?*
iuvenis	*young person*	**urbs**	*city*
meus	*my*	**venit**	*comes*

A mosaic of a theatre musician.

FELIX
Stage 6

1 amīcī per viam ambulābant.

2 canis subitō lātrāvit.

3 Caecilius canem timēbat.

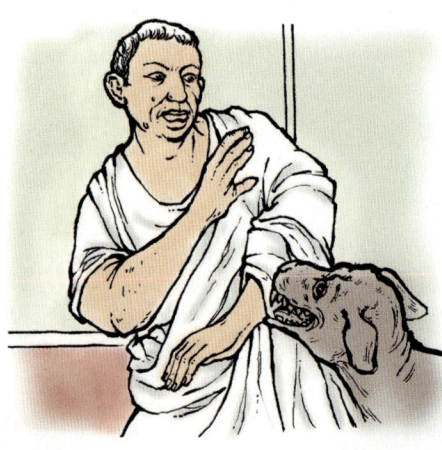

4 'pestis!' clāmāvit argentārius.

5 Barbillus erat fortis.

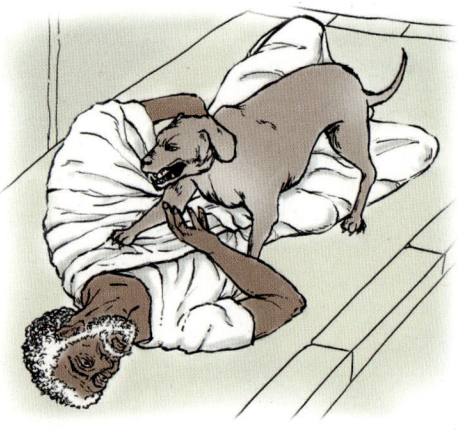

6 sed canis Barbillum superāvit.

7 Quīntus per viam ambulābat.

8 iuvenis clāmōrem audīvit.

9 canis Caecilium vexābat.

10 Quīntus canem pulsāvit.

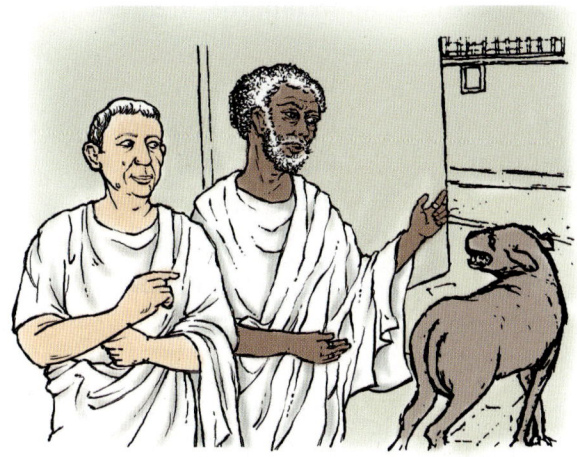

11 amīcī erant laetī.

12 amīcī Quīntum laudāvērunt.

pugna

Clēmēns in forō ambulābat. maxima turba erat in forō. servī et ancillae cibum emēbant. multī pistōrēs pānem vēndēbant. poēta recitābat.

    mercātor Graecus contentiōnem cum agricolā habēbat. mercātor īrātus pecūniam postulābat. subitō agricola mercātōrem pulsāvit, quod mercātor agricolam vituperābat. Pompēiānī rīdēbant, et agricolam incitābant.

    Clēmēns, postquam clāmōrem audīvit, ad pugnam festīnāvit. tandem agricola mercātōrem superāvit et ē forō agitāvit. Pompēiānī agricolam fortem laudāvērunt.

pugna *fight*	
maxima *very large*	
erat *was*	
pistōrēs *bakers*	
pānem vēndēbant	5
were selling bread	
contentiōnem habēbat	
was having an argument	
cum agricolā *with a farmer*	
postulābat *was demanding*	
pulsāvit *hit, punched*	10
quod *because*	
incitābant *were urging on*	
postquam *when, after*	
festīnāvit *hurried*	
superāvit *overpowered*	
agitāvit *chased*	

Fēlīx

multī Pompēiānī in tabernā vīnum bibēbant. Clēmēns tabernam intrāvit. subitō Clēmēns 'Fēlīx!' clāmāvit. Clēmēns Fēlīcem laetē salūtāvit. Fēlīx erat lībertus.

    Clēmēns Fēlīcem ad vīllam invītāvit. Clēmēns et Fēlīx vīllam intrāvērunt. Lūcia in ātriō stābat. Fēlīx Lūciam salūtāvit. Clēmēns Caecilium et Metellam quaesīvit. Caecilius in hortō legēbat. Metella in tablīnō scrībēbat. Caecilius et Metella ad ātrium festīnāvērunt et Fēlīcem salūtāvērunt.

    postquam Quīntus ātrium intrāvit, Fēlīx iuvenem spectāvit. lībertus erat valdē commōtus. paene lacrimābat, sed rīdēbat.

    tum Clēmēns ad culīnam festīnāvit. Grumiō in culīnā dormiēbat. Clēmēns coquum excitāvit et tōtam rem nārrāvit. coquus, quod erat laetus, cēnam optimam parāvit.

in tabernā *in an inn*	
laetē *happily*	
lībertus *freedman, ex-slave*	5
invītāvit *invited*	
valdē commōtus	
very moved, very shaken	
paene lacrimābat	
was almost crying	
tum *then*	10
excitāvit *woke up*	
tōtam rem nārrāvit	
told the whole story	
parāvit *prepared*	

Fēlīx et fūr

fūr *thief*

post cēnam Lūcia rogāvit, 'pater, cūr Fēlīx nunc est lībertus? ōlim erat servus tuus.'
   tum pater tōtam rem nārrāvit.

Caecilius: Fēlīx ōlim in tablīnō scrībēbat. Fēlīx erat sōlus. Clēmēns et Grumiō cibum in forō quaerēbant. Metella aberat, quod sorōrem vīsitābat.

Fēlīx: pater tuus aberat, quod argentāriam in forō administrābat.

Caecilius: nēmō erat in vīllā nisi Fēlīx et īnfāns. parvus īnfāns in cubiculō dormiēbat. subitō fūr per iānuam intrāvit. fūr tacitē ātrium circumspectāvit; tacitē cubiculum intrāvit, ubi īnfāns erat. Fēlīx nihil audīvit, quod intentē labōrābat. fūr parvum īnfantem ē vīllā tacitē portābat. subitō īnfāns vāgīvit. Fēlīx, postquam clāmōrem audīvit, statim ē tablīnō festīnāvit.

   'furcifer!' clāmāvit Fēlīx īrātus, et fūrem ferōciter pulsāvit. Fēlīx fūrem paene necāvit. ita Fēlīx parvum īnfantem servāvit.

Fēlīx: dominus, postquam rem audīvit, erat laetus et mē līberāvit. ego igitur sum lībertus.

Lūcia: sed quis erat īnfāns?

Caecilius: erat Quīntus!

post *after*
rogāvit *asked*
nunc *now*

ōlim *once, some time ago*
5   sōlus *alone*
aberat *was out*
sorōrem *sister*

administrābat *was managing*

nisi *except*
10   īnfāns *child, baby*
parvus *little*
tacitē *quietly, silently*
ubi *where*
nihil *nothing*
15   portābat *began to carry*
vāgīvit *wailed*
statim *at once*

necāvit *killed*
ita *in this way*
servāvit *saved*

20   līberāvit *freed, set free*
igitur *therefore, and so*

Felix.

About the language

1   All the stories in the first five Stages were written as if happening in the present, and in every sentence the verbs were in the **present tense**. Study the following examples:

PRESENT TENSE

singular	amīcus **labōrat**.	*The friend works* or *The friend is working.*
plural	amīcī **labōrant**.	*The friends work* or *The friends are working.*

2   In Stage 6, because the stories happened in the past, you have met the **imperfect tense** and the **perfect tense**. Study the different endings of the two past tenses and their English translation:

IMPERFECT TENSE

singular	poēta **recitābat**.	*A poet was reciting.*
	Metella in hortō **sedēbat**.	*Metella was sitting in the garden.*
plural	amīcī in forō **ambulābant**.	*The friends were walking in the forum.*
	Pompēiānī vīnum **bibēbant**.	*The Pompeians were drinking wine.*

PERFECT TENSE

singular	puella **intrāvit**.	*The girl entered.*
	Clēmēns clāmōrem **audīvit**.	*Clemens heard the noise.*
plural	amīcī Caecilium **salūtāvērunt**.	*The friends greeted Caecilius.*
	iuvenēs ad tabernam **festīnāvērunt**.	*The young people hurried to an inn.*

3   Compare the endings of the imperfect and perfect tenses with the endings of the present tense.

	singular	*plural*
PRESENT	portat	portant
IMPERFECT	portābat	portābant
PERFECT	portāvit	portāvērunt

You can see that in the imperfect and perfect tenses, as with the present tense, the singular ends in **-t** and the plural in **-nt**.

4   Notice how Latin shows the difference between 'is', 'are' and 'was', 'were'.

	singular	*plural*
PRESENT	Lūcia **est** in tablīnō.	fēminae **sunt** in hortō.
	Lucia is in the study.	*The women are in the garden.*
IMPERFECT	Lūcia **erat** in forō.	fēminae **erant** in viā.
	Lucia was in the forum.	*The women were in the street.*

5 In the following examples you will see that the imperfect tense is often used of an action or situation which was going on for some time.

īnfāns in cubiculō **dormiēbat**.
The baby was sleeping in the bedroom.

pater et māter **aberant**.
The father and mother were away.

6 The perfect tense, on the other hand, is often used of a completed action or an action that happened once.

agricola mercātōrem **pulsāvit**.
The farmer punched the merchant.

Pompēiānī agricolam **laudāvērunt**.
The Pompeians praised the farmer.

This richly decorated room full of mythological frescoes is from the House of the Vettii in Pompeii. The Vettii brothers were freedmen who became rich through trade and their house is one of the most lavish found in Pompeii.

Practising the language

avārus

	avārus *miser (stingy person)*

Two thieves pick an easy target: or so they think!

duo fūrēs ōlim ad vīllam contendēbant. in vīllā mercātor
habitābat. mercātor erat senex et avārus. avārus multam
pecūniam habēbat. fūrēs, postquam vīllam intrāvērunt,
ātrium circumspectāvērunt.

   'avārus,' inquit fūr, 'est sōlus. avārus servum nōn
habet.'

   tum fūrēs tablīnum intrāvērunt. avārus clāmāvit et
ferōciter pugnāvit, sed fūrēs senem facile superāvērunt.

   'ubi est pecūnia, senex?' rogāvit fūr.

   'servus fidēlis pecūniam in cubiculō custōdit,' inquit senex.

   'tū servum fidēlem nōn habēs, quod avārus es,'
clāmāvit fūr. tum fūrēs cubiculum petīvērunt.

   'pecūniam videō,' inquit fūr. fūrēs cubiculum
intrāvērunt, ubi pecūnia erat, et pecūniam intentē
spectāvērunt. sed ēheu! ingēns serpēns in pecūniā
iacēbat. fūrēs serpentem timēbant et ē vīllā celeriter
festīnāvērunt.

   in vīllā avārus rīdēbat et serpentem laudābat.

   'tū es optimus servus. numquam dormīs. pecūniam
meam semper servās.'

Glossary:
- **duo** *two*
- **habitābat** *was living*
- 5 **inquit** *said*
- **pugnāvit** *fought*
- **facile** *easily*
- 10 **fidēlis** *faithful*
- 15 **ingēns serpēns** *huge snake*
- **iacēbat** *was lying*
- **timēbant** *were afraid of, feared*
- **celeriter** *quickly*
- 20 **numquam** *never*
- **servās** *you look after, you keep safe*

---

1 Explore the story

a **duo fūrēs ōlim ad vīllam contendēbant. in vīllā mercātor habitābat** (lines 1–2):
who was hurrying to a merchant's house?

b **mercātor erat senex et avārus. avārus multam pecūniam habēbat** (lines 2–3):
what three things are we told about the merchant?

c **fūrēs, postquam vīllam intrāvērunt, ātrium circumspectāvērunt** (lines 3–4):
what did the thieves do after entering the house?

d **'avārus,' inquit fūr, 'est sōlus. avārus servum nōn habet'** (lines 5–6):
why did one of the thieves think the miser would be alone?

e **avārus clāmāvit et ferōciter pugnāvit, sed fūrēs senem facile superāvērunt** (lines 7–8): which two Latin words show the miser put up a fierce resistance to the thieves?

f **'servus fidēlis pecūniam in cubiculō custōdit,' inquit senex** (line 10): who did the old man say was guarding his money?

g **fūrēs cubiculum intrāvērunt, ubi pecūnia erat, et pecūniam intentē spectāvērunt** (lines 13–15): where did the thieves find the money?

h **ingēns serpēns in pecūniā iacēbat** (lines 15–16): what was lying on the money?

i **fūrēs serpentem timēbant et ē vīllā celeriter festīnāvērunt** (lines 16–17): why did the thieves leave the house in a hurry?

j **'tū es optimus servus. numquam dormīs. pecūniam meam semper servās'** (lines 19–20): what three things did the miser say in praise of the snake?

2 Explore the language

Look at these sentences from the story:

tum fūrēs tablīnum intrāvērunt. (line 7)

ingēns serpēns in pecūniā iacēbat. (lines 15–16)

> **imperfect tense** and **perfect tense:** page 88

The verbs in these sentences are in different tenses.

Explain how the different tenses change the meaning of each verb. You might want to use the words imperfect and perfect to refer to the tenses.

3 Explore further

Think about the whole story.

a What qualities of the snake did the old man praise?

b The old man called the snake an **optimus servus**. Does this story and the attitude of the old man fit with what you have learned about Roman attitudes towards enslavement?

ingēns serpēns.

Reviewing the language Stage 6: page 227

Enslaved people

Wherever you travelled in the Roman world, you would find people who had been enslaved like Grumio, Clemens and Melissa. While some people seem to have been concerned about the morality of enslavement, no serious attempt was made to abolish it. In this section we imagine how Melissa, Grumio and Felix might explain enslavement and freedom. In reality, however, we have very little evidence which tells us what enslaved people thought or felt about their lives, and the horror of enslavement is impossible to understand for those who have never experienced it.

Thinking point 1:
What do we mean when we say someone is 'enslaved'? Does enslavement still exist today?

> Since he bought me from Syphax, I am now considered to be the property of Caecilius. I have no choice in who owns me; I can be sold or given away as Caecilius wishes. Even my name can be changed if he chooses. I cannot marry or own personal possessions, and I can't seek the protection of the law courts.

The law did not even regard people like Melissa as human beings. Instead they were treated as property to be bought and sold.

Thinking point 2: The vocabulary at the back of this book gives two translations for **servus** (*male slave and enslaved man*) and **ancilla** (*female slave and enslaved woman*). The difference between these translations is important. The word 'slave' defines what a person like Melissa is, whereas 'enslaved' describes what has been *done to them*.

How might the choice of 'slave' or 'enslaved' change how we think about people like Melissa, Grumio and Clemens? What attitudes towards them might each choice reflect?

By the beginning of the first century AD there were perhaps as many as three enslaved people for every five free people in Italy. The Romans enslaved people of all races and cultures from all over the world: Gaul and Britain, Spain and North Africa, Egypt, different parts of Greece and Asia Minor, Syria and Palestine. The Romans often enslaved people who were taken as prisoners in war or captured by pirates. Families would be split up and people given new names. Children born to enslaved parents were automatically enslaved and could be bought and sold regardless of their parents' wishes.

Captured and enslaved men, women and children would be paraded as part of a victory procession ('triumph') through the streets of Rome. Images of bound captives destined for enslavement beneath a Roman trophy are common in art celebrating the military victories of the emperors. This example from the Temple of Apollo Sosianus in Rome shows a man and a woman, bound and seated on a platform ready to be lifted up and carried in a triumphal procession.

> **Thinking point 3:** Describe how the captives are depicted in this relief. What does this source tell you about the Roman attitudes to such people?

Some enslaved people were owned privately by a **dominus** like Caecilius. Others were owned publicly, by the town council, for example. Most Roman families owned at least one or two enslaved people. A merchant like Caecilius would have had no fewer than a dozen in his house and many more working on his estates and in his businesses. Very wealthy households kept hundreds, sometimes even thousands, of people in enslavement. A man called Pedanius Secundus had 400 enslaved people in his house in Rome; when one of them murdered him, they were all put to death, despite the protests of the people of Rome.

In the country enslaved people were made to work as shepherds and ranchers on big estates, labourers on farms, miners and builders of roads and bridges. Some of the strongest were bought for training as gladiators. In cities, enslaved people were used for a variety of skilled and unskilled work, including as cooks, gardeners, craftsmen and women, secretaries, musicians, actors and entertainers. Often free and enslaved people worked side by side, although a free person could choose to leave and earned a personal living from their work.

As shown in these pictures, enslaved people had to do a wide variety of work, from serving drinks in the home and nursing children, to heavy labour, such as transporting goods.

Thinking point 4: Think back over the previous Stages. What tasks have you seen being done by enslaved people?

Working in a household like Caecilius' is not as hard or dangerous as being down a mine or on a farm, but that doesn't mean it is easy. Metella as our domina keeps a close eye on the quality of my work, and if she doesn't like my cooking she can have me punished. A dominus or domina is free to beat those they enslave, and one common punishment is to be sent away to do much harder, more dangerous work on a farm or estate. I really don't want that!

I am free to move about the streets of the town. In fact, if someone met me on the street they might not realise I am enslaved; they might think I am a poor free man. I can go shopping, visit temples and attend performances at the theatre and amphitheatre. The big difference is that I can only do these things with the permission of Caecilius and Metella; I cannot choose how I spend my days.

Many enslaved people would have faced cruel and violent treatment in addition to the trauma of being enslaved. Roman law stated that someone had to have a 'good reason' to actually kill a person they held in enslavement, but in reality this provided little or no real protection for the enslaved. Enslaved people were considered to be the property of their dominus or domina, who controlled many aspects of their life, including access to necessities such as food, shelter or clothing. A dominus or domina might pay a large sum of money for a highly skilled enslaved person; for example, someone who could read and write, keep accounts, or manage the work of a small shop. Therefore, although they might try to keep them fit and healthy, they probably viewed them more as an investment than a fellow human being.

This mosaic from the Villa Romana del Casale in Sicily shows an enslaved man being beaten.

The Roman author Seneca records that a law was proposed requiring enslaved people to wear distinctive clothing so that they could be easily recognised. The lawmakers, however, realised that this meant that enslaved people might recognise *each other*, understand the strength of their numbers and rebel against those who held them in enslavement. The idea was abandoned.

Enslaved people may have been treated like property, but they did not simply obey unthinkingly. Acts of resistance might include completing tasks slowly or poorly, but there were also full-scale rebellions. In 73–71 BC the gladiator Spartacus famously led thousands of enslaved people in an armed uprising, which at one point threatened Rome itself.

Enslaved people also frequently tried to escape. The Romans called such people 'fugitives' (**fugitīvī** from the verb **fugit** meaning 'flees'), a word we still use today. Harbouring fugitives was a crime. Detailed descriptions of fugitives were put up in public places and rewards offered for their capture. Some people hired professional slave-hunters. A captured fugitive might have a brand or tattoo made on their face so everyone knew they had tried to escape.

> **Thinking point 5:** The word 'fugitive' reflects how the Romans thought about people who tried to escape from enslavement: they had broken the law and were criminals. Would such people have thought of themselves as a 'fugitive'? Can you think of an alternative term to use when referring to them?

In a letter to his friend, P. Rufus, the Roman politician Cicero appealed for his help locating an enslaved man who had escaped:

> **'Dionysius, an enslaved man of mine who looked after my library (and is worth a large sum of money), stole a large number of books and ran away to escape punishment. He is in your province. My friend Marcus Bolanus and many others saw him at Narona, but they believed him when he said I had given him his freedom. If you would take the trouble to return this man to me, I can't tell you how grateful I would be.'**
>
> **(Ad. Fam. 13.77.3)**

P. Rufus was the governor in charge of the area ('province') in which Cicero suspected Dionysius was hiding. Despite Cicero's political connections, however, Dionysius appears to have evaded capture.

> **Thinking point 6:** What may have been the challenges for a person like Dionysius trying to escape from enslavement?

Freedmen and freedwomen

The act of freeing an enslaved person was called **manūmissiō** (manumission). This word is connected with two other words, **manus** (hand) and **mittō** (send), and means 'a sending out from the hand' or 'setting free from control'. Manumission was performed in several ways. The oldest method took the form of a legal ceremony before a public official, such as a judge. This is the ceremony seen in the picture at the beginning of this Stage. A witness claimed that the enslaved person did not really belong to their dominus or domina, who did not deny this; then the enslaved person's head was touched with a rod and they were declared officially free. There were also other, simpler methods. A dominus or domina might manumit an enslaved person by making a declaration in the presence of friends at home or merely by an invitation to recline on the couch at dinner.

Sometimes, as in my case, freedom is given as a reward for a specific act or maybe for long service. While the law says they cannot own personal possessions, an enslaved person might amass assets such as money, goods and land that they can exchange for their freedom, although this is rare. People are also sometimes freed after the death of their dominus or domina by a statement in the will.

Most enslaved people will never be freed, however, and there are laws limiting who can be. For example, an enslaved person cannot be freed before the age of 30, and no more than 100 people (fewer in a small household) can be freed in a single will.

A man who has been freed, like me, is known as a **lībertus** (freedman). Freedmen can make their own way in life and might even become important members of the community; Caecilius' own father was actually a freedman. We do not, however, receive all the privileges of a citizen who was born free. We cannot stand as candidates in public elections or become high-ranking officers in the army.

Some freedmen continued to do the same work they did when enslaved or were set up in business by those who previously held them in enslavement. Others became priests in the temples or worked for the town council; the council secretaries, messengers, town clerk and town crier are all thought to have been freedmen. The architect who designed the large theatre in Pompeii was a freedman named Marcus Artorius Primus.

The peristylium of the House of the Vettii.

Some freedmen became very rich and powerful. The Vettii, two freedmen who were possibly brothers, owned one of the most magnificent houses in Pompeii.

Despite being free, I still have obligations to Caecilius. I have to work for him for a fixed number of days each year and am expected to help and support him whenever I can. I am one of his clients and visit him regularly to pay my respects, usually early in the morning for the salutatio. This connection is shown by my name: Caecilius' full name is Lucius Caecilius Iucundus, so now I am called Lucius Caecilius Felix.

A woman who had been freed from enslavement was called a **līberta**. Like freedmen, many freedwomen earned their living using the skills they had learnt while enslaved. Some stayed in the house where they had been enslaved and may have worked as hairdressers, seamstresses or nurses. Others are known to have worked as shopkeepers, artisans and even moneylenders. Some freedwomen married men who had previously held them in enslavement. We can never know the thoughts and feelings of these women, however, and therefore cannot make claims about whether they did so of their own free will.

Thinking point 7: How free were freedmen and freedwomen? What links and obligations did they have to the people who previously held them in enslavement?

Families might contain a mixture of free and enslaved people. We can see an example of one such family in the picture on the right of this page. In this memorial for a baby the names of the baby's father and grandparents suggest that the father was a freedman, while his parents were probably enslaved. The inscription reads:

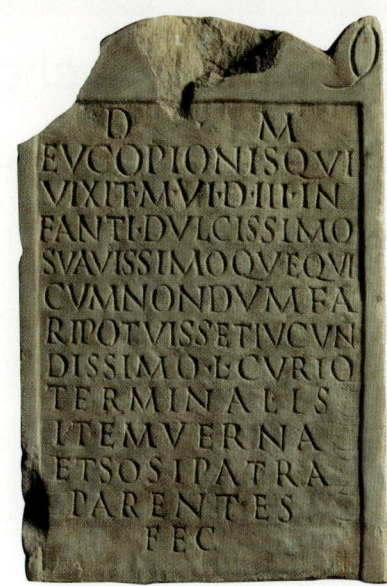

'To the memory of Eucopio, who died aged 6 months and 3 days.
   The sweetest, most pleasant and agreeable infant, even though he was not yet able to speak. Lucius Curio Terminalis, and his parents, Verna and Sosipatra, made this.'

> **Thinking point 8:** Think back to what you learned about Roman names in Stage 1. What about this inscription suggests that Lucius Curio Terminalis was free and that his parents were enslaved?

Enquiry: How much do we know about the lives of people enslaved by the Romans?

You may wish to consider the following:

- the types of work they did and their treatment
- acts of resistance
- how enslaved people were freed
- how the Romans thought about enslavement and enslaved people
- the limitations of the sources, including the lack of first-hand information from enslaved people themselves.

Vocabulary checklist 6

abest	*is out, is absent*	**postquam**	*when, after*
aberat	*was out, was absent*	**pulsat**	*hits, punches*
emit	*buys*	**quod**	*because*
ferōciter	*fiercely*	**rēs**	*thing*
festīnat	*hurries*	**scrībit**	*writes*
fortis	*brave, strong*	**subitō**	*suddenly*
fūr	*thief*	**superat**	*overcomes, overpowers*
intentē	*closely, carefully*	**tum**	*then*
lībertus	*freedman, ex-slave*	**tuus**	*your*
ōlim	*once, some time ago*	**vēndit**	*sells*
parvus	*small*	**vituperat**	*rebukes, tells off*
per	*through, along*		

A carved marble statue of the god Mithras killing a bull. The inscription reads:

'Alcimus, enslaved steward of Tiberius Claudius Livianus, gave this gift and fulfilled his vow to the sun-god Mithras.'

The worship of Mithras was especially popular among particular groups in Roman society, including enslaved people, freedmen, soldiers and officials who worked for the emperor.

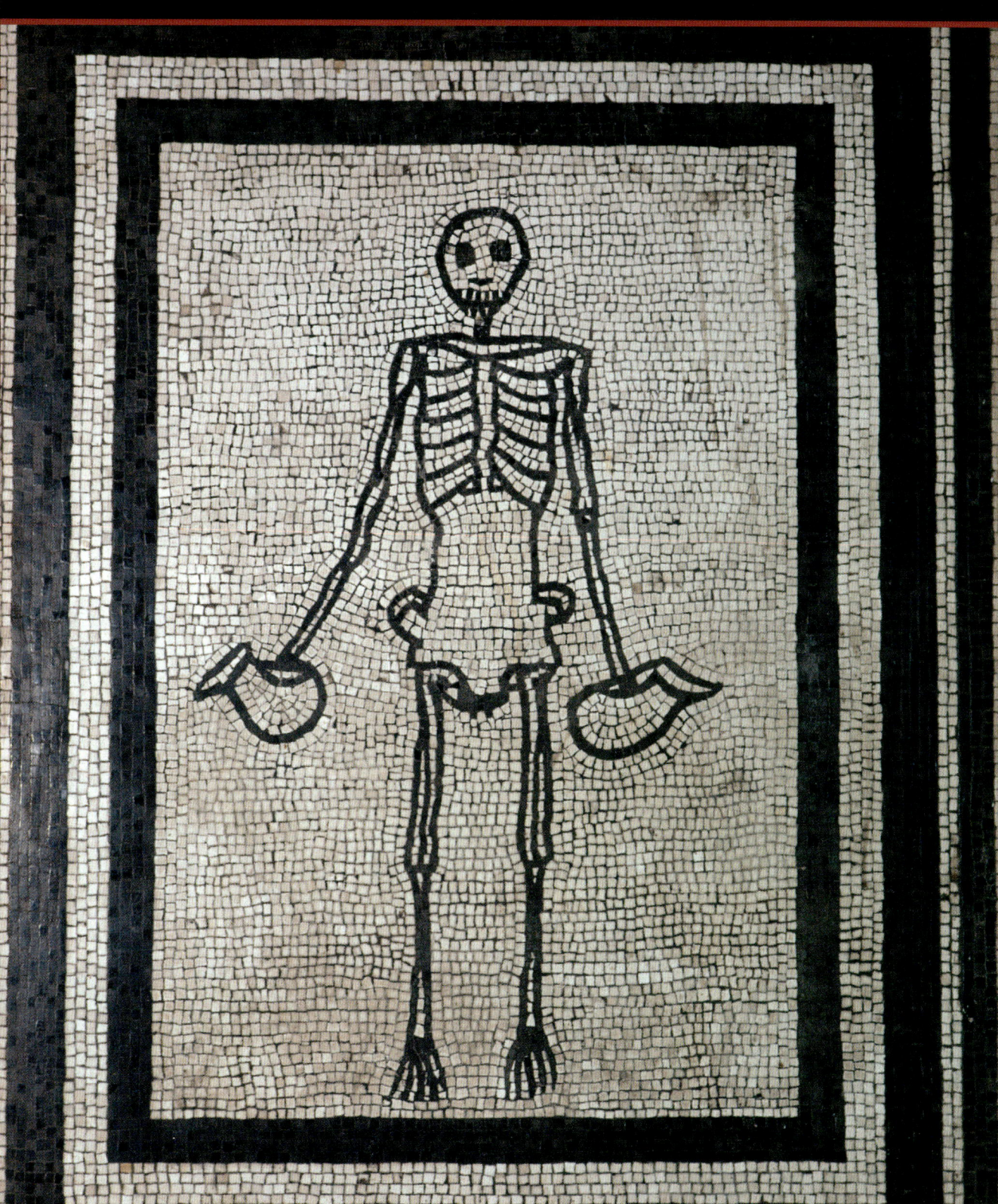

cēna

1 amīcus Caecilium vīsitābat.
vīllam intrāvit.

2 Caecilius amīcum exspectābat.
amīcum salūtāvit.

3 amīcus cum Caeciliō cēnābat.
cēnam laudāvit.

4 poēta trīclīnium intrāvit.
versum recitāvit.

5 amīcus pōculum īnspexit.
vīnum gustāvit.

6 amīcus pōculum hausit.
tum fābulam longam nārrāvit.

7 Caecilius plausit.
'euge!' dīxit.

8 amīcī optimum vīnum bibērunt.
tandem surrēxērunt.

9 servī in ātriō stābant.
iānuam aperuērunt.

10 amīcus 'valē' dīxit.
ē vīllā discessit.

fābula mīrābilis

multī amīcī cum Caeciliō et cum Metellā cēnābant. Fēlīx
quoque aderat. omnēs amīcī coquum laudāvērunt, quod
cēna erat optima.

postquam omnēs cēnāvērunt, Caecilius clāmāvit, 'ubi est
Decēns? Decēns nōn adest.'

tum Caecilius Clēmentem ē vīllā mīsit. servus Decentem
per urbem quaesīvit.

postquam servus ē vīllā discessit, Fēlīx pōculum hausit.
tum lībertus fābulam mīrābilem nārrāvit:

'ōlim amīcus meus ex urbe discēdēbat. nox erat, sed lūna
plēna lūcēbat. amīcus per viam festīnābat, ubi silva erat, et
subitō centuriōnem cōnspexit. amīcus meus centuriōnem
salūtāvit.

'centuriō tamen nihil dīxit. tum centuriō tunicam dēposuit.
ecce! centuriō ēvānuit. ingēns lupus subitō appāruit.

'amīcus meus valdē timēbat. ingēns lupus ululāvit et
ad silvam festīnāvit. tunica in viā iacēbat. amīcus tunicam
cautē īnspexit. ecce! tunica erat lapidea. tum amīcus rem
intellēxit. ille centuriō erat versipellis.'

mīrābilis
  extraordinary, strange

aderat *was there*

5

mīsit *sent*

discessit *departed, left*
pōculum hausit
  drained his cup
10 **ex urbe** *from the city*
nox erat *it was night*
lūna plēna *full moon*
lūcēbat *was shining*
silva *wood, forest*
centuriōnem cōnspexit
  caught sight of a centurion
dīxit *said*
tunicam dēposuit
  took off his tunic
ēvānuit *vanished*
lupus *wolf*
15 **appāruit** *appeared*
ululāvit *howled*
cautē *cautiously*
īnspexit *examined, inspected*
lapidea *made of stone*
rem intellēxit
  understood the truth
ille *that*
versipellis *werewolf*

About the language 1

1 Study the following example:

mercātor Caecilium vīsitābat. mercātor vīllam intrāvit.
A merchant was visiting Caecilius. The merchant entered the house.

2 In this Stage you met a shorter way of saying this:

mercātor Caecilium vīsitābat. vīllam intrāvit.
*A merchant was visiting Caecilius. **He** entered the house.*

The following sentences behave in the same way:

amīcī cum Caeciliō cēnābant. coquum laudāvērunt.
*Friends were dining with Caecilius. **They** praised the cook.*

Lūcia in ātriō stābat. amīcum salūtāvit.
*Lucia was standing in the atrium. **She** greeted the friend.*

3 Notice that Latin does not have to include a separate word for 'he', 'she' or 'they'. **intrāvit** can mean *he entered* or *she entered*, depending on the context.

4 Further examples:

  a Cerberus in culīnā stābat. cibum spectābat.

  b āctōrēs in theātrō clāmābant. fābulam agēbant.

  c Metella nōn erat in vīllā. in hortō ambulābat.

  d lībertī in tabernā bibēbant. Grumiōnem salūtāvērunt.

  e iuvenis pōculum hausit. vīnum laudāvit.

  f puellae in viā stābant. lupum audīvērunt.

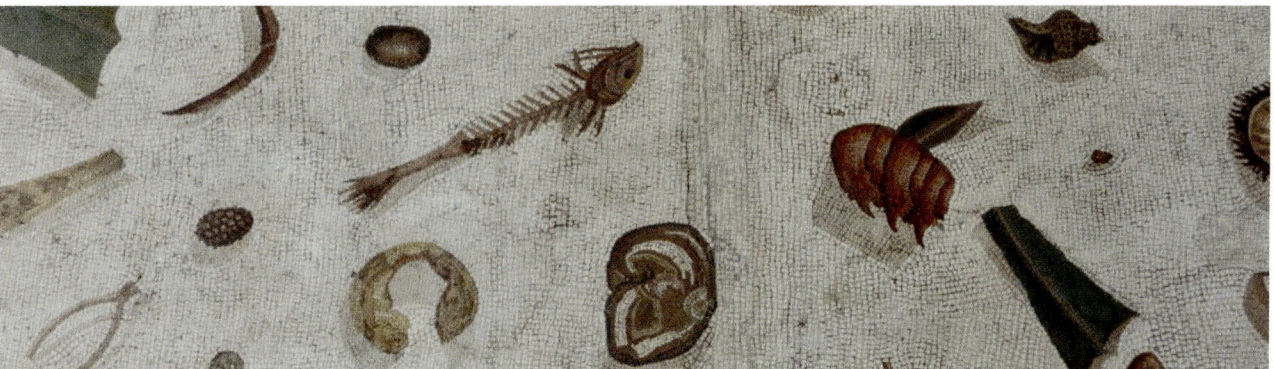

Part of a mosaic floor, showing the scraps left behind by the diners after a cena.

Decēns

postquam Fēlīx fābulam nārrāvit, omnēs plausērunt. tum hospitēs tacēbant et aliam fābulam exspectābant. subitō clāmōrem audīvērunt. omnēs ad ātrium festīnāvērunt, ubi Clēmēns stābat.

Caecilius:	hercle! quid est? cūr tū clāmōrem facis?	5
Clēmēns:	Decēns, Decēns . . .	
Caecilius:	quid est?	
Clēmēns:	Decēns est mortuus.	
omnēs:	quid? mortuus? ēheu!	
	(duo servī intrant.)	10
Caecilius:	quid dīcis?	
servus prīmus:	dominus meus ad vīllam tuam veniēbat; dominus gladiātōrem prope amphitheātrum cōnspexit.	
servus secundus:	gladiātor dominum terruit, quod ingentem gladium vibrābat. tum gladiātor clāmāvit, 'tū mē nōn terrēs, leō, tū mē nōn terrēs! leōnēs amīcum meum in arēnā necāvērunt, sed tū mē nōn terrēs!'	15
servus prīmus:	Decēns valdē timēbat. 'tū es īnsānus,' inquit dominus. 'ego nōn sum leō. sum homō.'	20
servus secundus:	gladiātor tamen dominum ferōciter petīvit et eum ad amphitheātrum trāxit. dominus perterritus clāmāvit. Clēmēns clāmōrem audīvit.	25
servus prīmus:	Clēmēns, quod fortis erat, amphitheātrum intrāvit. Decentem in arēnā cōnspexit. dominus meus erat mortuus.	
Metella:	ego rem intellegō! gladiātor erat Pugnāx. Pugnāx erat gladiātor nōtissimus. Pugnāx ōlim in arēnā pugnābat, et leō Pugnācem necāvit. Pugnāx nōn vīvit; Pugnāx est umbra. umbra Decentem necāvit.	30

plausērunt *applauded*
hospitēs *guests*
tacēbant
  became quiet, fell silent
aliam *another*
hercle!
  by Hercules! good heavens!

mortuus *dead*

prīmus *first*
gladiātōrem *gladiator*
prope amphitheātrum
  near the amphitheatre
secundus *second*
terruit *frightened*
gladium vibrābat
  was waving a sword
in arēnā *in the arena*
īnsānus *mad, crazy*

homō *human being, man*

eum *him*
trāxit *dragged*

nōtissimus *very famous*

vīvit *is alive*
umbra *ghost*

Decēns valdē timēbat.

post cēnam

postquam Metella rem explicāvit, omnēs amīcī tacēbant.
mox 'valē' dīxērunt et ē vīllā discessērunt. per viam timidē
prōcēdēbant. nūllae stēllae lūcēbant. nūlla lūna erat in caelō.
amīcī nihil audīvērunt, quod viae dēsertae erant. amīcī per
urbem tacitē prōcēdēbant, quod umbram timēbant.   5

explicāvit	*explained*
valē	*goodbye*
timidē	*nervously*
prōcēdēbant	
	were proceeding
nūllae stēllae	*no stars*
in caelō	*in the sky*
dēsertae	*deserted*

   subitō fēlēs ululāvit. amīcī valdē timēbant. omnēs per
urbem perterritī ruērunt, quod dē vītā dēspērābant. clāmōrem
mīrābilem fēcērunt. multī Pompēiānī erant sollicitī, quod
clāmōrem audīvērunt. Caecilius et Metella tamen clāmōrem
nōn audīverunt, quod in cubiculō dormiēbant.   10

fēlēs	*cat*
ruērunt	*rushed*
dē vītā dēspērābant	
	were in despair of their
	lives
fēcērunt	*made*
sollicitī	*troubled, anxious*

About the language 2

1   In Stage 6, you met examples of the perfect tense. They looked like this:

senex ad vīllam **ambulāvit**.   amīcī in tabernā **dormīvērunt**.
The old man walked to the house.   *The friends slept in the inn.*

This is a very common way of forming the perfect tense in Latin.

2   In this Stage, you have met other forms of the perfect tense.
Look at the following examples:

PRESENT	PERFECT	
	singular	*plural*
appāret	appāruit	appāruērunt
	s/he* appeared	*they appeared*
dīcit	dīxit	dīxērunt
	s/he said	*they said*
discēdit	discessit	discessērunt
	s/he left	*they left*
facit	fēcit	fēcērunt
	s/he made	*they made*

* 'it' and 'they' (singular) are also possible for any 's/he' form of the verb.

3   If you are not sure whether a particular verb is in the present tense or the
perfect tense, you can check by looking it up in the Vocabulary part of the
Language information section at the back of this book.

Dinner parties were a lot of work for the enslaved people of the household. They had to prepare and serve the food, look after the guests (including washing their feet), and of course clean up afterwards.

Melissa trīstis

trīstis *sad*

post cēnam Melissa erat occupāta. Clēmēns trīclīnium
intrāvit, ubi Melissa labōrābat. Melissa erat trīstis.
  'cūr tū es trīstis, Melissa?' rogāvit Clēmēns.
Melissa tamen nōn respondit. paene lacrimābat.
  Clēmēns ē trīclīniō discessit et ad culīnam festīnāvit, ubi   5
Grumiō labōrābat.
  'ego sum sollicitus,' inquit Clēmēns. 'Melissa est trīstis.'
  Grumiō et Clēmēns, postquam ē culīnā discessērunt,
trīclīnium intrāvērunt. Melissam vīdērunt. ēheu! Melissa   **vīdērunt** *saw*
lacrimābat.   10
  'Melissa, cūr lacrimās?' rogāvit coquus.
  'lacrimō quod ego sum sōla,' respondit Melissa.
  tum Melissa rem nārrāvit:
  'māter mea tabernam in Graeciā habēbat. pessimus vir   **pessimus vir** *very bad man*
ōlim tabernam intrāvit. māter erat occupāta, et vir mē   15
intentē spectābat. subitō vir manum meam cēpit et ē   **manum meam cēpit**
tabernā celeriter mē dūxit.'   *took my hand*
  'et māter tua?' rogāvit Grumiō. 'quid fēcit?'   **quid fēcit?** *what did she do?*
  'nihil vīdit,' respondit Melissa, 'quod magna turba erat in
tabernā. vir ad portum mē trāxit. ibi mē vēndidit. ego igitur   20   **ibi** *there*
sum ancilla sōla.'   **vēndidit** *sold*
  Grumiō erat valdē commōtus.   **sōla** *lonely*
  'fortasse tū es ancilla,' inquit coquus, 'sed nōn es sōla,   **fortasse** *perhaps*
quod amīcum habēs.'
  Clēmēns Grumiōnem spectāvit et 'ita vērō!' inquit,   25   **ita vērō** *yes*
'Herculēs adest!'

Practising the language

Lūcia callida

Lucia saves a cat and outwits a gladiator.

Lūcia et amīca prope amphitheātrum ambulābant.
subitō magnum clāmōrem audīvērunt et gladiātōrem
ēbrium cōnspexērunt. gladiātor fēlem agitābat.
 'tū mē nōn terrēs, leō!' clāmābat gladiātor. fēlēs
perterrita ululābat.   5
 'furcifer!' clāmāvit Lūcia. 'dēsiste!'
 gladiātor ēbrius Lūciam vīdit. gladium dēstrīnxit.
 'tū es puella stultissima,' inquit gladiātor. 'nēmō mē
impūne vexat.'
 tum gladiātor Lūciam ferōciter petēbat. fēlēs fūgit,   10
sed Lūcia immōta stābat. amīca valdē timēbat.
 'cavē!' clāmāvit Lūcia. 'umbra est in urbe!'
 'quid dīcis?' rogāvit gladiātor.
 'herī fūrēs tabernam intrāvērunt, ubi pistor
labōrābat, et pistōrem necāvērunt,' respondit Lūcia.   15
'nunc pistor est umbra. sed umbra nōn est contenta.
pistor fēlem habēbat. umbra igitur fēlem quaerit.'
 gladiātor perterritus fūgit.
 'umbra est in urbe?' rogāvit amīca. 'nunc intellegō!
Lūcia, callida es!'   20

callida *clever*

amīca *friend*

ēbrium *drunk*

dēsiste! *stop!*
dēstrīnxit *drew out*
stultissima *very foolish*
impūne *safely*
fūgit *ran away, fled*
immōta *still, motionless*
cavē! *beware!*

herī *yesterday*

contenta *satisfied*

1 Explore the story

a Lūcia et amīca prope amphitheātrum ambulābant. subitō magnum clāmōrem audīvērunt et gladiātōrem ēbrium cōnspexērunt (lines 1–3):
what two things did Lucia and her friend do while walking near the amphitheatre?

b 'tū mē nōn terrēs, leō!' clāmābat gladiātor (line 4):
what did the gladiator seem to think the cat was?

c fēlēs perterrita ululābat (lines 4–5):
what was the cat doing while the gladiator was shouting at it?

d gladiātor ēbrius Lūciam vīdit. gladium dēstrīnxit (line 7):
what did the gladiator do after he saw Lucia?

e tum gladiātor Lūciam ferōciter petēbat. fēlēs fūgit, sed Lūcia immōta stābat. amīca valdē timēbat (lines 10–11).
Why do you think Lucia's friend was so frightened?

f 'herī fūrēs tabernam intrāvērunt, ubi pistor labōrābat, et pistōrem necāvērunt' (lines 14–15): which of the following claims did Lucia make?

    A Yesterday thieves entered a shop and killed a baker.

    B Yesterday thieves entered a shop and a baker killed them.

g 'nunc pistor est umbra. sed umbra nōn est contenta' (line 16):
what two things are we told about the ghost?

h 'pistor fēlem habēbat. umbra igitur fēlem quaerit' (line 17):
what did Lucia say the ghost was doing, and why?

i gladiātor perterritus fūgit (line 18): what did the gladiator do?

j 'umbra est in urbe?' rogāvit amīca. 'rem intellegō! Lūcia, callida es!' (lines 19–20):
write down the Latin word that indicates what the friend thought of Lucia.
Do you agree with her?

2 Explore the language

a Find a sentence where there is a verb in the perfect tense.

b Find a sentence where there is a verb in the imperfect tense.

> imperfect tense and perfect tense: page 88

c Find a sentence where there is a verb in the present tense.

3 Explore further

Think about the whole story and what you have learned about Roman beliefs concerning life after death.

Why do you think the gladiator was **perterritus**?

Reviewing the language Stage 7: page 228

Roman beliefs about death and burial

Tombs outside the Herculaneum Gate.

The Romans usually placed the tombs of the dead by the roadside just outside towns. The tombs at Pompeii can still be seen along the roads that go north from the Herculaneum Gate and south from the Nuceria Gate.

Some tombs were grand and looked like small houses; others were plain and simple. In the first century AD the bodies of those who had died were often burned and their ashes collected. This is called cremation. If they could afford it, a person's ashes were placed inside a tomb in a chest or vase, which could be made of various materials, including stone, metal and glass. Sometimes there were recesses set into the walls of a tomb to hold the remains of several members of a family. The ashes of people who could not afford an expensive tomb were buried more simply, for example, in an old storage jar buried in the earth.

One Pompeian had his ashes buried in this fabulously expensive, hand-carved blue and white glass vase, which was found in one of the tombs outside the Herculaneum Gate.

Inside a Pompeian tomb, with recesses for the ashes.

Thinking point 1: Look at the images of tombs and urns on these pages. What claims can we make about the people buried in each of these?

Many poorer people put the ashes of the dead in second-hand storage jars which were then buried in the earth.

A name scratched into a Pompeii city wall. Sometimes the dead were buried in small urns along the wall and their name engraved above the burial spot.

This tomb is that of Eumachia, the patron of the clothworkers, who paid for the construction of the largest building in Pompeii's forum.

Unless the dead are properly treated, their spirits might haunt and possibly harm the living, like what happened to poor Decens. Therefore, it is very important to provide the dead with a tomb or grave as a suitable home for their ghosts. The dead like to be close to the living, so that they aren't forgotten and can keep an eye on things. This is why we build cemeteries along busy roads, rather than in peaceful and secluded places. This is reflected in the inscriptions on some of the tombs, for example:

> 'I see and gaze upon all who come to and from the city.'

> 'Lollius has been placed by the side of the road in order that everyone who passes may say to him "Hello, Lollius".'

Tombs also remind any passer-by of the prestige and wealth of the deceased individuals, and of course that of their surviving family!

When the bodies of the dead are cremated some of their possessions might be burned or buried with them. People also tend to be identified on their gravestones with objects that were important to them when they were alive. A craftsperson might want to be depicted with their tools or the things they made, or, at the very least, have their occupation inscribed on their tomb.

Thinking point 2: Think back to the story of Decens being killed by a vengeful ghost. Why might Caecilius' guests have believed such a story to be true?

Thinking point 3: Why do you think some people burned or buried the possessions of the deceased with their body? Why might someone want their craft mentioned on their memorial?

Stone burial urn of Sellia Epyre from Rome: cut into the top is her profession, 'maker of gold-threaded dresses'.

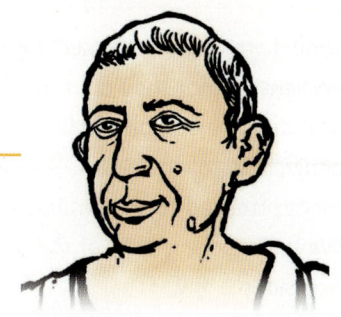

The ghosts of the dead get hungry and thirsty. Things like eggs, beans, lentils, flour and wine are placed regularly at the tomb; sometimes holes are made so that food and wine can be poured inside. Blood is the favourite drink of the dead, but wine is a good substitute. At the funeral and on special occasions, animals like pigs and chickens are sacrificed, their blood offered and the meat left for the dead to enjoy in the afterlife.

A Roman poet called Propertius related how the ghost of his girlfriend Cynthia appeared to him one night as he slept:

> **'She had the same hair as when she was carried to the grave, the same eyes, but the side of her dress was singed and the fire had destroyed the ring she usually wore on her finger . . .'**

(Propertius 4.7)

Cynthia complained that he had not given her a proper funeral; he had not accompanied her funerary procession to the graveside and had not provided wine or flowers for her burial. She requested certain things for her grave, including an inscription –

> **'worthy of me but brief, suitable for a traveller to read as he hurries from Rome'**

– and the planting of ivy. She also asked that Propertius look after her nurse and free her favourite enslaved woman. Her ghost would not be content unless he did as he was told.

Section through a Roman burial in Caerleon, Wales. A pipe ran down into the container for the ashes so that gifts of food and drink could be poured in.

Thinking point 4: What claims can we make about Roman beliefs about life after death, using the image of the burial in Caerleon and Propertius' poem?

Tombs are often decorated with flowers and surrounded by little gardens so that they are a pleasant place to be. Family and friends of a dead person also hold a banquet after the funeral and on the anniversary of the death. Sometimes these take place in a dining room attached to the tomb itself, sometimes in the family home. We believe the ghosts of the dead attend and enjoy these cheerful occasions.

In addition to these banquets, two festivals for the dead are held every year. At the **parentālia**, families remember parents and relations who have died. At the **lemūria**, we perform rites to exorcise any ghosts in our houses, who might be lonely or hungry and therefore dangerous.

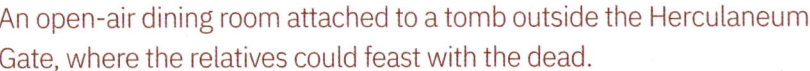

An open-air dining room attached to a tomb outside the Herculaneum Gate, where the relatives could feast with the dead.

Some people also believed in the Greek myths about the underworld, where the wicked were punished for their crimes, while the good might live happily forever.

'Mystery religions' (so called because of their very secretive teachings, of which little evidence remains) were popular in the Greek and Roman worlds. One example is the cult of the Egyptian goddess Isis, popular all over the Roman world. Cults like this were often based on sacred stories involving the death and return of a powerful figure, and it is thought that one of the benefits of belonging to such a religious group was the promise of a better afterlife.

A bronze head of Epicurus, from a villa at Herculaneum.

Fresco from the Temple of Isis in Herculaneum showing a sacrifice in progress attended by worshippers.

There were a few people who did not believe in any form of life after death. Amongst these were the followers of a Greek philosopher called Epicurus, who taught that when a person died the breath that gave them life dissolved in the air and was lost forever.

Most Romans, however, felt no need to question their traditional beliefs and customs, which kept the dead alive in their memories and ensured that their spirits were happy and at peace.

> **Thinking point 5:** How do Roman beliefs and practices relating to death, burial and life after death compare with those you know of from different times and places?

Enquiry: To what extent were Roman burial customs more for the living than for the dead?

You may wish to consider the following:

- location and nature of tombs
- how the body was treated and what was buried with it
- inscriptions on tombs and urns
- Roman beliefs in life after death.

Vocabulary checklist 7

cōnspicit: cōnspexit	*catches sight of*	**nihil**	*nothing*
cum	*with*	**omnis**	*all*
facit: fēcit	*makes, does*	**parat: parāvit**	*prepares*
herī	*yesterday*	**prope**	*near*
ingēns	*huge*	**rogat: rogāvit**	*asks*
intellegit: intellēxit	*understands*	**surgit: surrēxit**	*gets up, rises*
lacrimat: lacrimāvit	*weeps, cries*	**tacitē**	*quietly, silently*
mortuus	*dead*	**tamen**	*however*
nārrat: nārrāvit	*tells, relates*	**terret: terruit**	*frightens*
necat: necāvit	*kills*	**valdē**	*very much, very*

This relief is from a Roman sarcophagus and shows three figures from Greek mythology who were infamous for their eternal punishment in the afterlife: Tantalus was always thirsty no matter how much he drank; Ixion was tied to an ever-revolving wheel; and Sisyphus was forced to forever roll a boulder up a hill.

amphitheātrum

1 nūntiī spectāculum nūntiābant.
Pompēiānī nūntiōs audiēbant.

2 gladiātōrēs per viam prōcēdēbant.
Pompēiānī gladiātōrēs laudābant.

3 puellae iuvenēs salūtāvērunt.
iuvenēs quoque ad amphitheātrum
contendēbant.

4 mercātōrēs fēminās spectābant, quod fēminae ad spectāculum contendēbant.

5 puerī per viam festīnābant. puellae puerōs salūtāvērunt.

6 Pompēiānī tabernās nōn intrāvērunt, quod tabernae erant clausae.

7 postquam gladiātōrēs Pompēiānōs salūtāvērunt, Pompēiānī plausērunt.

8 Pompēiānī gladiātōrēs intentē spectābant, quod gladiātōrēs in arēnā pugnābant.

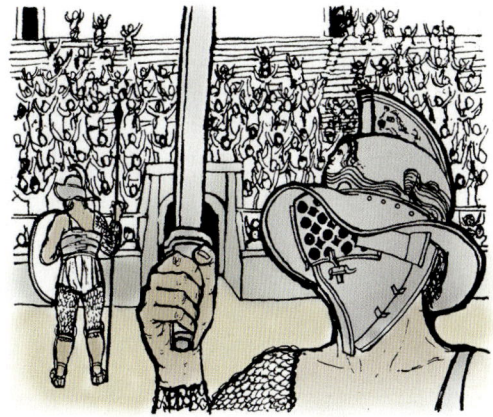

9 spectātōrēs murmillōnēs incitābant, quod murmillōnēs saepe victōrēs erant.

gladiātōrēs

spectātōrēs amphitheātrum Pompēiānum complēbant. Rēgulus pugnās ēdēbat, quod diem nātālem celebrābat. Rēgulus erat senātor Rōmānus, et prope Nūceriam habitābat. Nūcerīnī amphitheātrum nōn habēbant. multī Nūcerīnī igitur in amphitheātrō Pompēiānō erant.

tuba sonuit. duo rētiāriī et duo murmillōnēs arēnam intrāvērunt. murmillōnēs Pompēiānōs valdē dēlectābant, quod saepe victōrēs erant; sed Nūcerīnī rētiāriōs incitābant.

murmillōnēs rētiāriōs frūstrā ad pugnam prōvocāvērunt. rētiāriī, quod erant expedītī, murmillōnēs facile ēvītāvērunt.

'rētiāriī sunt ignāvī!' clāmāvērunt Pompēiānī. Nūcerīnī tamen respondērunt, 'rētiāriī murmillōnēs dēcipiunt!'

tum murmillō clāmāvit, 'ūnus murmillō facile duōs rētiāriōs superat.'

postquam Pompēiānī plausērunt, murmillō rētiāriōs statim petīvit. murmillō et rētiāriī ferōciter pugnāvērunt. tandem rētiāriī murmillōnem graviter vulnerāvērunt. tum rētiāriī alterum murmillōnem petīvērunt. hic murmillō fortiter pugnāvit, sed rētiāriī eum quoque superāvērunt.

Pompēiānī, quod īrātī erant, murmillōnēs vituperābant; missiōnem tamen postulābant, quod murmillōnēs fortēs erant. Nūcerīnī mortem postulābant. omnēs spectātōrēs tacēbant, et Rēgulum intentē spectābant. Rēgulus pollicem vertit. Pompēiānī erant īrātī, et vehementer clāmābant. rētiāriī tamen, postquam Rēgulus signum dedit, murmillōnēs interfēcērunt.

complēbant	*were filling*
ēdēbat	*was presenting*
diem nātālem celebrābat	
	was celebrating his birthday
5 **senātor Rōmānus**	
	Roman senator
tuba	*trumpet*
sonuit	*sounded*
rētiāriī	*retiarii*
10	*(gladiators with nets)*
murmillōnēs	*murmillones*
	(heavily armed gladiators)
saepe	*often*
victōrēs	*victors, winners*
15 **frūstrā**	*in vain*
prōvocāvērunt	*challenged*
expedītī	*lightly armed*
ēvītāvērunt	*avoided*
ignāvī	*cowardly*
20 **dēcipiunt**	
	are deceiving, are fooling
ūnus	*one*
graviter	*seriously*
vulnerāvērunt	*wounded*
25 **alterum**	*the second, the other*
hic	*this*
fortiter	*bravely*
missiōnem	*release*
mortem	*death*
pollicem vertit	
	turned his thumb up
vehementer	
	loudly, energetically
signum dedit	*gave the signal*
interfēcērunt	*killed*

A retiarius with his trident, net and protection for his right arm and neck.

About the language 1

1   From Stage 2 onwards, you have met sentences like these:

amīcus **puellam** salūtat.   *The friend greets the girl.*

coquus **amīcum** vīsitābat.   *The cook was visiting his friend.*

nautae **mercātōrem** laudāvērunt.   *The sailors praised the merchant.*

In each of these examples, the person who has something done to him or her is indicated in Latin by the **accusative singular**.

nominative case and accusative case: page 25

2   In Stage 8, you have met sentences like these:

amīcus **puellās** salūtat.   *The friend greets the girls.*

coquus **amīcōs** vīsitābat.   *The cook was visiting his friends.*

nautae **mercātōrēs** laudāvērunt.   *The sailors praised the merchants.*

In these examples, the persons who have something done to them are indicated in Latin by the **accusative plural**.

3   You have now met the following cases:

SINGULAR

| *nominative* | puella | amīcus | mercātor |
| *accusative* | puellam | amīcum | mercātōrem |

PLURAL

| *nominative* | puellae | amīcī | mercātōrēs |
| *accusative* | puellās | amīcōs | mercātōrēs |

4   Further examples:

a   nauta gladiātōrem laudāvit. nauta gladiātōrēs laudāvit.

b   amīcus nautam vituperābat. amīcus nautās vituperābat.

c   centuriō amīcōs laudāvit.

d   puer āctōrēs ad theātrum dūxit.

e   senex āctōrem ad forum dūxit.

f   amīcus fābulās nārrāvit.

g   fēminae cibum gustāvērunt.

h   agricolae nūntiōs audīvērunt.

The amphitheatre at Pompeii. Notice one of the staircases that led up to the top seats. The public sports ground is behind the trees on the right. On performance days, the open space would have been full of stalls selling refreshments and souvenirs.

vēnātiō

vēnātiō *hunt*

When you have read this story, answer the questions at the end.

postquam rētiāriī ex arēnā discessērunt, tuba iterum sonuit. subitō multī cervī arēnam intrāvērunt. cervī per tōtam arēnam currēbant, quod perterritī erant. tum canēs ferōcēs per portam intrāvērunt. canēs statim cervōs perterritōs agitāvērunt et interfēcērunt. 5

postquam canēs cervōs superāvērunt, lupī arēnam intrāvērunt. lupī, quod valdē ēsuriēbant, canēs ferōciter petīvērunt. canēs erant fortissimī, sed lupī facile canēs superāvērunt.

Nūcerīnī erant laetissimī et Rēgulum laudābant. 10 Pompēiānī tamen nōn erant contentī, sed clāmābant, 'ubi sunt leōnēs? cūr Rēgulus leōnēs retinet?'

Rēgulus, postquam hunc clāmōrem audīvit, signum dedit. statim trēs leōnēs per portam ruērunt. tuba iterum sonuit. bēstiāriī arēnam audācissimē intrāvērunt. leōnēs tamen 15 bēstiāriōs nōn petīvērunt. leōnēs in arēnā recubuērunt. leōnēs obdormīvērunt!

tum Pompēiānī erant īrātissimī, quod Rēgulus spectāculum rīdiculum ēdēbat. Pompēiānī Rēgulum et Nūcerīnōs ex amphitheātrō agitāvērunt. Nūcerīnī per viās 20 fugiēbant, quod valdē timēbant. Pompēiānī tamen gladiōs cēpērunt et multōs Nūcerīnōs interfēcērunt.

ecce! sanguis nōn in arēnā sed per viās fluēbat.

iterum *again*
cervī *deer*
ferōcēs *fierce, ferocious*

ēsuriēbant *were hungry*
fortissimī *very brave*

contentī *satisfied*
retinet *is holding back*
hunc *this*
trēs *three*
bēstiāriī *beast fighters*
audācissimē *very boldly*
recubuērunt *lay down*
obdormīvērunt *went to sleep*
īrātissimī *very angry*
spectāculum rīdiculum *ridiculous spectacle*
fugiēbant *began to run away, began to flee*

Questions

1   postquam rētiāriī ex arēnā discessērunt, tuba iterum sonuit. subitō multī cervī arēnam intrāvērunt (lines 1–2): what two things happened after the net fighters left the arena?

2   canēs statim cervōs perterritōs agitāvērunt et interfēcērunt (lines 4–5): which one of the following statements is true?

   A   The dogs terrified the deer before chasing them.

   B   The dogs terrified the deer before killing them.

   C   The dogs chased the deer before killing them.

   D   The dogs chased the deer but did not kill them.

3   lupī, quod valdē ēsuriēbant, canēs ferōciter petīvērunt. canēs erant fortissimī, sed lupī facile canēs superāvērunt (lines 7–9): what two things are we told about the wolves?

4   Nūcerīnī erant laetissimī et Rēgulum laudābant (line 10): write down the Latin word that indicates how the Nucerians were feeling about the hunt.

5   Look at lines 11–12 (Pompēiānī tamen nōn erant contentī, sed clāmābant, 'ubi sunt leōnēs? cūr Rēgulus leōnēs retinet?'). Why do you think the Pompeians were not satisfied with the hunt?

6   statim trēs leōnēs per portam ruērunt. tuba iterum sonuit. bēstiāriī arēnam audācissimē intrāvērunt (lines 14–15): which two groups were next to go into the arena?

7   leōnēs tamen bēstiāriōs nōn petīvērunt. leōnēs in arēnā recubuērunt. leōnēs obdormīvērunt! (lines 15–17): what three things are we told about the lions?

8   tum Pompēiānī erant īrātissimī, quod Rēgulus spectāculum rīdiculum ēdēbat. Pompēiānī Rēgulum et Nūcerīnōs ex amphitheātrō agitāvērunt (lines 18–20): what happened after the Pompeians became very angry?

9   Pompēiānī tamen gladiōs cēpērunt et multōs Nūcerīnōs interfēcērunt (lines 21–22): write down the Latin word that shows how many Nucerians were killed.

10   Look at line 23 (ecce! sanguis nōn in arēnā sed per viās fluēbat). Why do you think that ecce! has been put in front of the last sentence?

About the language 2

1 Study the following pairs of sentences:

Pompēiānī erant īrātī.   Pompēiānī erant **īrātissimī**.
The Pompeians were angry.   *The Pompeians were very angry.*

gladiātor est nōtus.   gladiātor est **nōtissimus**.
The gladiator is famous.   *The gladiator is very famous.*

māter erat laeta.   māter erat **laetissima**.
The mother was happy.   *The mother was very happy.*

The words in **bold** are known as **superlatives**. Notice how they are translated in the examples above.

2 Further examples:

a mercātor est trīstis. senex est trīstissimus.

b canis erat ferōx. leō erat ferōcissimus.

c fīlia fābulam longissimam nārrāvit.

d murmillōnēs erant fortēs, sed rētiāriī erant fortissimī.

Gladiator fights were intended to be an entertaining spectacle and were performed to the sound of trumpet and organ, as shown in this section of a mosaic depicting gladiator fights and hunts from a Roman villa in Nennig, Germany.

Quīntus audāx

audāx *bold*

Caecilius et Quīntus in tablīnō sedēbant. Caecilius fīlium ad vēnātiōnem invītāvit.

'aper ferōcissimus in monte Vesuviō habitat,' inquit Caecilius. 'multī cīvēs ad vēnātiōnem veniunt. servī et canēs sunt parātī. Fēlīx quoque venit, quod audāx est. aper eum nōn terret.'

Quīntus erat laetissimus. vēnābulum cēpit et ad vēnātiōnem contendit. omnēs ad montem prōcēdēbant, ubi aper habitābat. mox magnam silvam intrāvērunt. servī canēs incitāvērunt. canēs vehementer lātrābant.

subitō ingēns aper appāruit. Caecilium et cīvēs terruit. Fēlīx vēnābulum ēmīsit, sed aprum nōn percussit. lībertus, quod aper eum petēbat, dē vītā dēspērābat. omnēs valdē timēbant. Quīntus tamen ad aprum fortiter prōcessit et vēnābulum ēmīsit. ecce! aprum necāvit.

'euge!' clāmāvit Quīntus. 'ōlim Fēlīx mē servāvit. nunc ego Fēlīcem servō!'

aper ferōcissimus
  very fierce boar

5 **in monte Vesuviō**
  on Mount Vesuvius
cīvēs *citizens*
vēnābulum *hunting spear*

10

ēmīsit *threw*
percussit *struck*
prōcessit *advanced*

15

Practising the language

Androclus et leō

How a lion saved the life of a condemned man.

ōlim Androclus per silvam currēbat. Androclus
erat fugitīvus. subitō Androclus leōnem cōnspexit.
leō tamen Androclum nōn agitāvit. leō lacrimābat!
Androclus erat attonitus et rogāvit,
    'cūr lacrimās, leō? cūr mē nōn agitās? cūr mē nōn   5
cōnsūmis?'
    leō trīstis pedem ostendit. Androclus spīnam in pede
cōnspexit.
    'ego spīnam videō!' exclāmāvit Androclus. 'ingentem
spīnam videō! nunc intellegō! tū lacrimās, quod pēs   10
dolet.'
    Androclus, quod benignus et fortis erat, ad leōnem
cautē vēnit et spīnam īnspexit. tum clāmāvit, 'leō! ego
perterritus sum, sed tē adiuvō.'
    postquam hoc dīxit, Androclus spīnam quam   15
celerrimē extrāxit. leō ē silvā festīnāvit.
    mox Rōmānī Androclum comprehendērunt, et
eum ad arēnam dūxērunt. postquam arēnam intrāvit,
Androclus spectātōrēs vīdit et valdē timēbat. tum
Androclus bēstiās vīdit et clāmāvit, 'nunc mortuus   20
sum! ecce! bēstiae! videō leōnēs et lupōs. ēheu!'
    tum ingēns leō ad eum ruit. leō, postquam
Androclum olfēcit, nōn eum cōnsūmpsit sed lambēbat!
Androclus attonitus leōnem agnōvit et dīxit,
    'tē agnōscō! tū es leō trīstis! spīna erat in pede tuō.'   25
    posteā, Rōmānī attonitī Androclum et leōnem
līberāvērunt.

fugitīvus *fugitive
(from enslavement)*
attonitus *astonished*

pedem ostendit
showed its paw
spīnam *thorn*
exclāmāvit *exclaimed*
dolet *hurts*
benignus *kind*
vēnit *came*
adiuvō *I help*
hoc *this*
quam celerrimē
as quickly as possible
extrāxit *pulled out*
comprehendērunt *arrested*
bēstiās *wild animals*

olfēcit *smelled, sniffed*
lambēbat *began to lick*
agnōvit *recognised*
posteā *afterwards*

Mosaic of a lion from the bath complex in the
city of Uzitta in modern Tunisia, North Africa.

1 Explore the story

a **ōlim Androclus per silvam currēbat. Androclus erat fugitīvus** (lines 1–2): why was Androclus running through a forest?

b **Androclus erat attonitus et rogāvit, 'cūr lacrimās, leō? cūr mē nōn agitās? cūr mē nōn cōnsūmis?'** (lines 4–6): what three things did Androclus ask the lion?

c **'nunc intellegō! tū lacrimās, quod pēs dolet'** (lines 10–11): according to Androclus, why was the lion crying?

d **Androclus, quod benignus et fortis erat, ad leōnem cautē vēnit et spīnam īnspexit** (lines 12–13): write down the Latin word that shows why Androclus was prepared to approach the lion and inspect the thorn.

e **tum clāmāvit, 'leō! ego perterritus sum, sed tē adiuvō'** (lines 13–14): what two things did Androclus shout to the lion?

f Which is the correct translation of **leō ē silvā festīnāvit** (line 16)?

    A The lion hurries out of the wood.

    B The lion was hurrying out of the wood.

    C The lion hurried out of the wood.

    D The lion hurried through the wood.

g **mox Rōmānī Androclum comprehendērunt, et eum ad arēnam dūxērunt** (lines 17–18): think about the whole story and explain why the Romans led Androclus to the arena.

h **postquam arēnam intrāvit, Androclus spectātōrēs vīdit et valdē timēbat** (lines 18–19): how did Androclus feel after he entered the arena and saw the spectators?

i **tum Androclus bēstiās vīdit et clāmāvit, 'nunc mortuus sum!'** (lines 19–21): what two things did Androclus then do?

j **leō, postquam Androclum olfēcit, nōn eum cōnsūmpsit sed lambēbat** (lines 22–23): what two things happened after the lion smelled Androcles?

2 Explore the language

a Look at lines 9–10: **'ingentem spīnam videō! nunc intellegō!'** Explain why these verbs end in **-ō**.

b Explain why the accusatives **leōnēs** (line 21) and **leōnem** (line 24) have different endings.

> **verb endings:** page 56
> **accusative case:** page 123

3 Explore further

Think about the whole story and then reread what Androclus says.

a How does the way Androclus talks in lines 5–6 show us that he is confused?

b How does the way Androclus talks in lines 20–21 show us that he is afraid?

Reviewing the language Stage 8: page 230

Gladiatorial shows

Public games, including gladiator fights, were held in the amphitheatre and watched by huge crowds of excited spectators. Pompeii's amphitheatre was probably large enough to contain the whole population of the town as well as many visitors from nearby.

Soon after dawn on the day of a show the audience begin to take their places. A trumpet blares and priests come out to perform a religious ceremony to mark the beginning of the games.

We enter in procession, parade around the arena, and salute the sponsor of the show. Then we are paired off to fight. Gladiators live and train together in a 'school' or barracks under the supervision of a professional trainer. It's possible, therefore, that you'll be paired up to fight against a friend.

While some gladiators are free volunteers, most are enslaved, condemned criminals or prisoners of war who do not have a choice in whether or not they fight. Fights end when one of us either dies or surrenders.

Thinking point 1:
Why might a religious ceremony be performed at the start of the games?

The inside of the Pompeii amphitheatre as it is today.

Diagram of Pompeii's amphitheatre.

The Flavian Amphitheatre (also known as the Colosseum) in Rome is one of the most famous venues for gladiatorial games, but the remains of amphitheatres can be found all over the Roman Empire, from Pompeii to Caerleon in Wales. The amphitheatre at Pompeii was a large oval building without a roof, in which rising tiers of seats surrounded an arena. As in the theatre, large pieces of canvas (awnings) were spread over part of the seating area to give shelter from the sun, and it is unclear whether women sat apart from men.

> **Thinking point 2:** Based on these details about the amphitheatres, what claims can we make about the popularity of entertainment like gladiatorial games in the Roman world?

Spectators paid no admission fee, as the shows were given by wealthy individuals at their own expense. The shows – and their sponsors – were advertised in signs painted on walls all over Pompeii such as this one:

> '**Twenty pairs of gladiators, given by Lucretius Satrius Valens, priest of Nero, and ten pairs of gladiators provided by his son will fight at Pompeii from 8 to 12 April. There will also be an animal hunt. Awnings will be provided.**'

The illustrations here, based on a relief from the tomb of a wealthy Pompeian, show a defeated gladiator appealing to the spectators; the victor stands by ready to kill him if they decide that he deserves to die. Notice the arm raised in appeal. The spectators indicated their wishes by turning their thumbs up or down: probably turning the thumb up towards the chest meant 'kill him,' while turning it down meant 'let him live,' although this is not known for certain. The final decision for death or mercy was made by the sponsor of the show.

> **Thinking point 3:** Why might a wealthy individual pay for gladiatorial shows? Why might someone want images such as those above on their tomb?

It's actually quite likely that your life will be spared if you lose, especially if you are well known and have won some impressive victories in the past. The most successful gladiators are great favourites with the crowd and even receive gifts of money from their admirers. One popular Pompeian gladiator is described as 'the girls' heartthrob,' and I've even heard of gladiator sweat being sold as a souvenir!

Eventually, if you survive long enough or show great skill and courage, you might be awarded the wooden sword. This is a high honour and means you don't have to fight again.

We know that doctors were employed to stitch up wounded gladiators – the famous doctor Galen wrote that he particularly enjoyed doing this work in AD 157–161 as he got to look inside human bodies! – but we cannot know for sure how gladiators handled what must have been life-changing injuries. The Romans did make things like artificial limbs and walking aids, but it was probably only the rich who could afford them.

Types of gladiator

Gladiators were not all armed in the same way. Many examples of gladiators' armour with traces of fabrics embroidered with gold thread were discovered at Pompeii.

Samnite

Eques

Thracian

Dimachaerus

Murmillo

Retiarius

Secutor

- Some, who were known as **Samnites**, carried an oblong shield and a short sword.
- Others, known as **Thracians**, had a round shield and a curved sword or dagger.
- Another type of gladiator armed with sword and shield wore a helmet with a crest shaped like a fish; the Greek name for the fish was 'mormillos' and the gladiator was known as a **murmillō**.
- The murmillones were often matched against the **rētiāriī**, who were armed with **rētia** (nets) and three-pronged tridents.
- Other types of gladiator fought with spears, on horseback, or from chariots

Part of the programme of one particular show, together with details of the results, reads as follows:

'A Thracian versus a Murmillo
Won: Pugnax from Nero's school: 3 times a winner
Died: Murranus from Nero's school: 3 times a winner

A Heavily Armed Gladiator versus a Thracian
Won: Cycnus from the school of Julius: 8 times a winner
Allowed to live: Atticus from the school of Julius: 14 times a winner

Chariot Fighters
Won: Scylax from the school of Julius: 26 times a winner
Allowed to live: Publius Ostorius: 51 times a winner'

> **Thinking point 4:**
> Consider the story **gladiātōrēs.** Why might murmillones be matched against the retiarii? Who do you think had the greater advantage in the arena?

From left to right: a retiarius' neck guard, two helmets, a greave (leg protector) and a shield.

Female gladiators might be uncommon, but we do exist! Some people don't like it, though, and there have been laws passed to regulate us: for example, one forbidding freeborn women under the age of 20 from taking part in gladiatorial games.

I was trained by my father. Some women have private lessons with a gladiator trainer. We don't train with or fight the men, but if we impress the audience we can still be rewarded with fame, fortune and a lifestyle which 'respectable' women could only dream of!

There must have either been a significant number of freeborn women choosing to fight in the arena or a few who were very prominent; if there were not, the law mentioned by the gladiator (passed in AD 11 by the Roman Senate) would not have been thought necessary. We cannot know why such women might have given up any claim to 'respectability' for the danger of the arena. Some may have wanted excitement; others may have been desperate to escape debt. It is worth noting that the law only refers to 'freeborn' women, so it can be assumed that an enslaved woman might still have been forced to fight. In fact, the inscription on the relief of Amazon and Achilia reads

> **'they were freed,'**

suggesting that these were enslaved women who won their freedom with their performances. Emperor Septimius Severus banned women's participation in the arena in AD 200.

> **Thinking point 5:**
> Why might a freeborn woman choose to fight in the arena? Why is it impossible to know for sure, and what problems does this cause for historians?

First–second century AD marble relief of female gladiators from Halicarnassus (modern Turkey). Their names are given as Amazon and Achillia, suggesting they may have been restaging the legendary fight between Achilles and the Amazonian queen, Penthesiliea, at Troy.

Animal hunts

Many shows also offered a **vēnātiō**, a hunt of wild animals. The **bēstiae** (wild beasts), such as wolves, wild boar, hares and lions, were released from cages into the arena, where they were hunted by specially trained beast fighters called **bēstiāriī**. The hunters wore light clothing and relied upon their spear and agility to avoid injury. By the end of the hunt all the animals, and occasionally a few hunters, had been killed.

These shows were designed to showcase the superiority of human skill and discipline over (untamed) nature. The traffic in exotic animals for slaughter in the arena was an empire-wide business.

Detail from a fresco which decorated a handrail in the theatre in Mérida, Spain.

> **Thinking point 6:** Can you think of any other examples of people fighting animals for entertainment like this? Does it still happen today? What do you think about such practices?

Thinking point 7: This illustration is based on a wall painting from Pompeii and shows lots of stalls set up around the amphitheatre; you might see something similar at a modern sports ground or stadium. Why do you think people set up stalls around the amphitheatre? What might they be selling?

The riot at Pompeii

The story told in this Stage is based on an actual event which occurred in AD 59. In addition to the evidence given in the wall painting shown here, the event is also described by the Roman historian Tacitus:

> 'About this time, a slight incident led to a serious outburst of rioting between the people of Pompeii and Nuceria. It occurred at a show of gladiators, sponsored by Livineius Regulus. While hurling insults at each other, in the usual manner of country people, they suddenly began to throw stones as well. Finally, they drew swords and attacked each other. The men of Pompeii won the fight. As a result, most of the families of Nuceria lost a father or a son. Many of the wounded were taken to Rome, where the Emperor Nero requested the Senate to hold an inquiry. After the inquiry, the Senate forbade the Pompeians to hold such shows for ten years. Livineius and others who had encouraged the riot were sent into exile.'

(Annals XIV.17)

This drawing of a gladiator with the palm of victory was scratched on a wall, with a message that may refer to the riot and its aftermath: 'Campanians, in your moment of victory you perished along with the Nucerians.'

Thinking point 8: What claims about gladiatorial shows can we make, using this source? Consider ideas such as the nature and behaviour of the audience and the importance of these shows to the Romans.

Enquiry: 'The Romans attended the amphitheatre to watch men kill each other in pursuit of glory.' To what extent do you agree with this claim?

You may wish to consider the following:

- Was attending the amphitheatre just about entertainment?
- Was man vs man combat the only type of show that people could watch?
- Did all gladiators fight for glory? Were there other motivations?

Vocabulary checklist 8

agitat: agitāvit	*chases, hunts*	**pēs**	*foot*
cōnsūmit: cōnsūmpsit	*eats*	**porta**	*gate*
dūcit: dūxit	*leads, takes*	**postulat: postulāvit**	*demands*
eum	*him*	**puer**	*boy*
facile	*easily*	**pugnat: pugnāvit**	*fights*
ferōx	*fierce, ferocious*	**saepe**	*often*
gladius	*sword*	**sanguis**	*blood*
hic	*this*	**signum**	*seal, signal, sign*
ignāvus	*cowardly*	**silva**	*wood, forest*
leō	*lion*	**statim**	*at once*
nūntius	*messenger*	**tōtus**	*whole*

This marble carving was found on a tomb believed to be that of the politician Gnaeus Alleius Nigidius Maius. We know he was well known for organising events at the amphitheatre, as his name appears in many of the adverts around Pompeii.

THERMAE

Stage 9

1 Quīntus ad thermās vēnit.

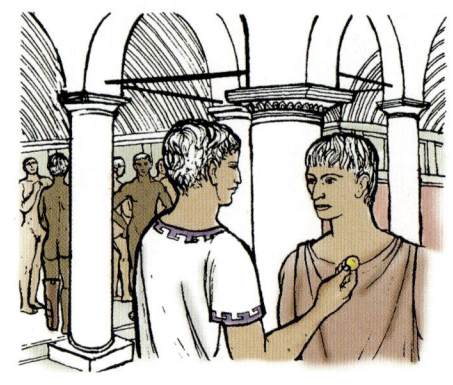

2 Quīntus servō pecūniam dedit.

3 amīcī Quīntum laetē salūtāvērunt,
quod diem nātālem celebrābat.

4 amīcī, postquam apodytērium intrāvērunt,
tunicās dēpōnēbant.

5 amīcī in caldāriō sedēbant. servī amīcīs
oleum et strigilēs ferēbant.

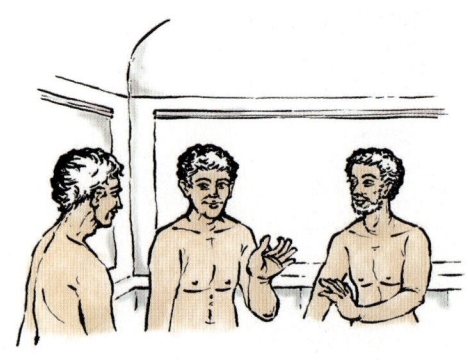

6 euge! thermae amīcōs valdē
dēlectābant.

7 Metella et Melissa in forō ambulābant.
Metella fīliō dōnum quaerēbat.

8 fēminae mercātōrem cōnspexērunt.
mercātor fēminīs togās ostendit.

9 Metella Quīntō togam ēlēgit. Melissa
mercātōrī pecūniam dedit.

10 Grumiō cēnam optimam in culīnā
parābat. coquus Quīntō cēnam parābat.

11 multī hospitēs cum Quīntō cēnābant.
Clēmēns hospitibus vīnum offerēbat.

12 Poppaea trīclīnium intrāvit. Quīntus
Poppaeae signum dedit. ancilla suāviter
cantāvit.

in palaestrā

When you have read this story, answer the questions opposite.

Caecilius Quīntō discum dedit, quod diem nātālem celebrābat.
tum Caecilius fīlium ad thermās dūxit, ubi palaestra erat.
servus Quīntō discum ferēbat.

Caecilius et fīlius, postquam thermās intrāvērunt, ad
palaestram contendērunt. ingēns turba in palaestrā erat.   5
Quīntus multōs iuvenēs et āthlētās cōnspexit. Quīntus multās
statuās in palaestrā vīdit.

'Pompēiānī āthlētīs nōtissimīs statuās posuērunt,' inquit
Caecilius.

in palaestrā erat porticus longa. spectātōrēs in porticū   10
stābant. servī spectātōribus vīnum offerēbant.

Quīntus turbam prope porticum vīdit. ingēns āthlēta in
mediā turbā stābat.

'quis est āthlēta ille?' rogāvit Quīntus.

'ille est Milō, āthlēta nōtissimus,' respondit Caecilius.   15
Caecilius et Quīntus ad Milōnem contendērunt.

Quīntus āthlētae discum novum ostendit. Milō, postquam
discum īnspexit, ad mediam palaestram prōcessit. āthlēta
palaestram circumspectāvit et discum ēmīsit. discus longē
per aurās ēvolāvit. spectātōrēs āthlētam laudāvērunt. servus   20
Milōnī discum quaesīvit. servus, postquam discum invēnit,
ad Milōnem rediit. servus āthlētae discum offerēbat. āthlēta
tamen discum nōn accēpit.

'discus nōn est meus,' inquit Milō.

servus Quīntō discum trādidit. tum iuvenis quoque discum   25
ēmīsit. discus iterum per aurās ēvolāvit. discus tamen
statuam percussit.

'ēheu!' clāmāvit Caecilius. 'statua nāsum frāctum habet.'

Quīntus rīdēbat. Pompēiānī rīdēbant. Milō tamen nōn
rīdēbat.   30

'cūr tū nōn rīdēs?' rogāvit iuvenis.

Milō erat īrātissimus.

'pestis!' respondit āthlēta. 'mea est statua!'

---

in palaestrā
in the palaestra, in the exercise area

discum *discus*
thermās *baths*
ferēbat *was carrying*

āthlētās *athletes*
statuās *statues*
posuērunt *have put up*

porticus longa
long colonnade
offerēbant *were offering*
in mediā turbā
in the middle of the crowd

novum *new*

longē *a long way, far*
per aurās ēvolāvit
flew through the air
invēnit *found*
rediit *went back*
nōn accēpit *did not accept*
meus *mine*
trādidit *handed over*

nāsum frāctum *broken nose*

Questions

1. **Caecilius Quīntō discum dedit, quod diem nātālem celebrābat** (line 1): why did Caecilius give Quintus a discus?

2. **tum Caecilius fīlium ad thermās dūxit, ubi palaestra erat** (line 2): where was the exercise area located?

3. **ingēns turba in palaestrā erat. Quīntus multōs iuvenēs et āthlētās cōnspexit** (lines 5–6): what two groups of people did Quintus see in the crowd in the exercise area?

4. **'Pompēiānī āthlētīs nōtissimīs statuās posuērunt,' inquit Caecilius** (lines 8–9): write down the two Latin words that indicate who the Pompeians put the statues up for.

5. Look at lines 12–15 (**Quīntus turbam prope porticum vīdit. ingēns āthlēta in mediā turbā stābat.**

   'quis est āthlēta ille?' rogāvit Quīntus.

   'ille est Milō, āthlēta nōtissimus,' respondit Caecilius). Write down two Latin words that describe the athlete Milo.

6. **Quīntus āthlētae discum novum ostendit. Milō, postquam discum īnspexit, ad mediam palaestram prōcessit** (lines 17–18): what two things did Milo do after Quintus showed him his new discus?

7. **āthlēta palaestram circumspectāvit et discum ēmīsit. discus longē per aurās ēvolāvit. spectātōrēs āthlētam laudāvērunt** (lines 18–20): what two things happened when Milo threw the discus?

8. **servus Milōnī discum quaesīvit. servus, postquam discum invēnit, ad Milōnem rediit. servus āthlētae discum offerēbat. āthlēta tamen discum nōn accēpit** (lines 20–23): which two of the following statements are true?

   A The slave looked for the discus.

   B The slave did not find the discus.

   C The slave offered Milo the discus.

   D Milo accepted the discus.

9. **tum iuvenis quoque discum ēmīsit. discus iterum per aurās ēvolāvit. discus tamen statuam percussit** (lines 25–27): what two things happened when Quintus threw the discus?

10. Look at lines 28–33 (**'ēheu!' clāmāvit Caecilius . . . 'pestis!' respondit āthlēta. 'mea est statua!'**). Write down one Latin word that shows how Caecilius felt, and do the same for Quintus, the Pompeians and Milo.

The palaestra of the Stabian Baths at Pompeii.

About the language

1 Study the following examples:

Metella **fīliae** cibum offerēbat.
*Metella was offering food **to her daughter**.*

senex **amīcō** dōnum quaerēbat.
*The old man was looking for a gift **for his friend**.*

Caecilius **mercātōrī** statuam ēmit.
*Caecilius bought a statue **for the merchant**.*

māter **puellīs** pecūniam trādidit.
*The mother handed over money **to the girls**.*

Quīntus **amīcīs** discum ostendit.
*Quintus showed the discus **to his friends**.*

iuvenēs **leōnibus** cibum dedērunt.
*The young men gave food **to the lions**.*

The Latin words in **bold** are nouns in the **dative case**.

2 You have now met three cases. Notice the different ways in which they are used:

nominative   **amīcus** dormiēbat.
              The friend *was sleeping.*

accusative   mercātor **amīcum** excitāvit.
              *The merchant woke **the friend**.*

dative   mercātor **amīcō** signum dedit.
              *The merchant gave a sign **to the friend**.*

3 Here is a full list of the noun endings that you have met. The new datives are in **bold**.

	first declension	*second declension*	*third declension*
SINGULAR			
nominative	puella	amīcus	mercātor
accusative	puellam	amīcum	mercātōrem
dative	**puellae**	**amīcō**	**mercātōrī**
PLURAL			
nominative	puellae	amīcī	mercātōrēs
accusative	puellās	amīcōs	mercātōrēs
dative	**puellīs**	**amīcīs**	**mercātōribus**

4 Further examples:

  a amīcus Caeciliō vīnum ostendit.

  b agricola uxōrī ānulum ēmit.

  c mercātor Metellae togam trādidit.

  d senex gladiātōribus pecūniam offerēbat.

  e fēmina fīliīs tunicās quaerēbat.

5 Notice the different cases of the words for 'I' and 'you':

nominative	ego	tū
accusative	mē	tē
dative	mihi	tibi

ego senem salūtō.   *I greet the old man.*

senex **mē** salūtat.   *The old man greets **me**.*

senex **mihi** statuam ostendit. *The old man shows a statue **to me**.*

tū pictūram pingis.   ***You** are painting a picture.*

āthlēta **tē** laudat.   *The athlete praises **you**.*

āthlēta **tibi** pecūniam dat.   *The athlete gives money **to you**.*

in tabernā

Metella et Melissa ē vīllā māne discessērunt. Metella fīliō togam
quaerēbat. Metella et ancilla, postquam forum intrāvērunt,
tabernam cōnspexērunt, ubi togae optimae erant. multae
fēminae erant in tabernā. servī fēminīs stolās ostendēbant. duo
gladiātōrēs quoque in tabernā erant. servī gladiātōribus tunicās 5
ostendēbant. mercātor in mediā tabernā stābat. mercātor erat
Marcellus.

Marcellus: quid quaeris, domina?

Metella: togam quaerō. ego fīliō dōnum quaerō, quod
diem nātālem celebrat. 10

Marcellus: ego multās togās habeō.

mercātor servīs signum dedit. servī mercātōrī togās celeriter
trādidērunt. Marcellus fēminīs togās ostendit. Metella et ancilla
togās īnspexērunt.

Melissa: ecce! hae togae sunt sordidae! 15

(*Marcellus servōs vituperāvit.*)

Marcellus: sunt intus togae splendidae.

Marcellus fēminās intus dūxit. mercātor fēminīs aliās togās
ostendit. Metella Quīntō mox togam splendidam ēlēgit.

Metella: haec toga, quantī est? 20

Marcellus: quīnquāgintā dēnāriōs cupiō.

Melissa: quīnquāgintā dēnāriōs cupis! furcifer! ego tibi
decem dēnāriōs offerō.

Marcellus: quadrāgintā dēnāriōs cupiō.

Melissa: tibi quīndecim dēnāriōs offerō. 25

Marcellus: quid? haec est toga pulcherrima! quadrāgintā
dēnāriōs cupiō.

Metella: tū nimium postulās. ego tibi trīgintā dēnāriōs dō.

Marcellus: cōnsentiō.

(*Melissa Marcellō pecūniam dedit. Marcellus* 30
Metellae togam trādidit.)

Marcellus: ego tibi maximās grātiās agō, domina.

māne *in the morning*
togam *toga*

domina *madam, my lady*
dōnum *present, gift*
hae *these*
sordidae *dirty, filthy*
intus *inside*
splendidae *splendid*
aliās *other*
ēlēgit *chose*
haec *this*
quantī est? *how much is it?*
quīnquāgintā dēnāriōs
     fifty denarii
decem *ten*
quadrāgintā *forty*
quīndecim *fifteen*
pulcherrima *very beautiful*
nimium *too much*
trīgintā *thirty*
cōnsentiō *I agree*
tibi maximās grātiās agō
     thank you very much

A fabric shop.

in apodytēriō

duo servī in apodytēriō stant. servī sunt Sceledrus et Anthrāx.

Sceledrus: cūr nōn labōrās, Anthrāx? num dormīs?

Anthrāx: quid dīcis? dīligenter labōrō. ego cīvibus togās custōdiō.

Sceledrus: togās custōdīs? mendāx es! 5

Anthrāx: cūr mē vituperās? mendāx nōn sum. togās custōdiō.

Sceledrus: tē vituperō, quod fūr est in apodytēriō, sed tū nihil facis.

Anthrāx: ubi est fūr? fūrem nōn videō. 10

Sceledrus: ecce! homō ille est fūr. fūrem facile agnōscō.

(Sceledrus Anthrācī fūrem ostendit. fūr togam suam dēpōnit et togam splendidam induit. servī ad fūrem statim currunt.)

Anthrāx: quid facis? furcifer! haec toga nōn est tua! 15

fūr: mendāx es! mea est toga! abī!

Sceledrus: tē agnōscō! pauper es, sed togam splendidam geris.

(mercātor intrat. togam frūstrā quaerit.)

mercātor: ēheu! ubi est toga mea? toga ēvānuit! 20

(mercātor circumspectat.)

ecce! hic fūr togam meam gerit!

fūr: parce! parce! pauperrimus sum . . . uxor mea est aegra . . . decem līberōs habeō . . .

mercātor et servī fūrem nōn audiunt, sed eum ad iūdicem trahunt. 25

---

in apodytēriō
in the changing room

num dormīs?
surely you are not asleep?
dīligenter *carefully*

suam *his*
induit *is putting on*

abī! *go away!*

pauper *poor*
geris *are wearing*

parce! *have pity!*
pauperrimus *very poor*
aegra *sick, ill*
līberōs *children*

This mosaic of a squid is in an apodyterium in Herculaneum.

Left: the caldarium (hot room) in the Forum Baths, Pompeii. At the nearer end note the large rectangular marble bath, which was filled with hot water. At the far end there is a stone basin for cold water. Rooms in baths often had grooved, curved ceilings to channel condensation down the walls.
Right: an apodyterium (changing room) in the women's section of the Stabian Baths at Pompeii. The alcoves in the walls are for people to store their clothes.

Practising the language

thermae

Typical activities at the baths in Pompeii.

cīvēs Pompēiānī trēs thermās habēbant. cīvēs cotīdiē ad thermās ībant. servī post dominōs ambulābant. servī dominīs oleum et strigilēs ferēbant.

cīvēs et servī, postquam thermās intrāvērunt, āthlētās et pugilēs vidēbant. āthlētae per palaestram currēbant 5 et saliēbant. servī āthlētīs tunicās tenēbant. aliī servī pugilibus follēs tenēbant. pugilēs follēs vehementer pulsābant.

cīvēs in palaestrā quoque sē exercēbant. multī discōs ēmittēbant. servī cīvibus discōs quaerēbant. servī, 10 postquam discōs invēnērunt, ad cīvēs reveniēbant. tum servī cīvibus discōs trādēbant.

cīvēs, postquam sē exercuērunt, apodytērium intrābant. omnēs in apodytēriō togās dēpōnēbant, et tepidārium intrābant. cīvēs in tepidāriō paulīsper 15 sedēbant, tum ad caldārium ībant. in caldāriō erant multae sellae. ibi dominī sedēbant et garriēbant. servī dominōs dīligenter rādēbant. thermae Pompēiānōs valdē dēlectābant.

ībant	*used to go*
oleum	*oil*
strigilēs	*strigils, scrapers*
pugilēs	*boxers*
follēs	*punchballs*
sē exercēbant	*were exercising*
tepidārium	*warm room*
paulīsper	*for a short time*
caldārium	*hot room*
garriēbant	*were chatting, were gossiping*
rādēbant	*were scraping*

1 **Explore the story**

a **cīvēs Pompēiānī trēs thermās habēbant** (line 1): how many sets of baths did the Pompeians have?

b **cīvēs cotīdiē ad thermās ībant** (lines 1–2): how often did Pompeian citizens go to the baths?

c **servī post dominōs ambulābant. servī dominīs oleum et strigilēs ferēbant** (lines 2–3): what two things did enslaved people do on the way to the baths?

d **cīvēs et servī, postquam thermās intrāvērunt, āthlētās et pugilēs vidēbant** (lines 4–5): which two groups of people did the citizens and the enslaved people see once they were inside the baths?

e **servī, postquam discōs invēnērunt, ad cīvēs reveniēbant. tum servī cīvibus discōs trādēbant** (lines 10–12): what two things did the enslaved people do after they found the discuses?

f **omnēs in apodytēriō togās dēpōnēbant, et tepidārium intrābant. cīvēs in tepidāriō paulīsper sedēbant, tum ad caldārium ībant** (lines 14–16): which two of the following statements are true?

   A Everyone undressed in the changing room before going into the warm room.

   B Everyone went through the warm room before undressing in the changing room.

   C Citizens stood for a short time in the hot room before going into the warm room.

   D Citizens sat for a short time in the warm room before going into the hot room.

g **in caldāriō erant multae sellae. ibi dominī sedēbant et garriēbant** (lines 16–17): write down two Latin words that indicate there was lots of room to sit down in the hot room.

h **servī dominōs dīligenter rādēbant** (lines 17–18): describe what the enslaved people did in the hot room.

i Write down an English word that comes from **diligenter** (line 18).

2 **Explore the language**

Look again at these two sentences:
    servī cīvibus discōs quaerēbant. (line 10)
    tum servī cīvibus discōs trādēbant. (lines 11–12)
What is different about the way you translate the dative **cīvibus** in each of these sentences?

— dative: page 144

3 **Explore further**

a As well as bathing, what other activities did the Pompeians enjoy at the baths in the story?

b Think about what you have learned about the Roman baths in this Stage and reread the final sentence (**thermae Pompēiānōs valdē dēlectābant**). Do you think that this sentence is true for everyone living in Pompeii?

Reviewing the language Stage 9: page 231

The baths

The vast majority of Pompeians did not have bathrooms in their houses; they went regularly to the public baths to keep themselves clean. Bath houses have been found all over the empire, many of which seem to have been built using money donated by rich individuals. Archaeologists have found four bath complexes in Pompeii; the Stabian Bath (the oldest), the Forum Baths, the Sarno Baths and the Central Baths (still being built at the time of the eruption).

The baths acted as a hub for business and political engagement. As with a modern leisure centre or health club, people could exercise, meet friends and have a snack there. Not all baths charged entry fees and they were open to all free people, so bathing would have meant mingling with people from all classes.

Thinking point 1:
You have seen other examples of public buildings funded by rich Romans; can you remember any? (Think back to the forum in Stage 4.) Why might a wealthy Roman pay for a grand public building like a bath house?

Plan of the Forum Baths, Pompeii

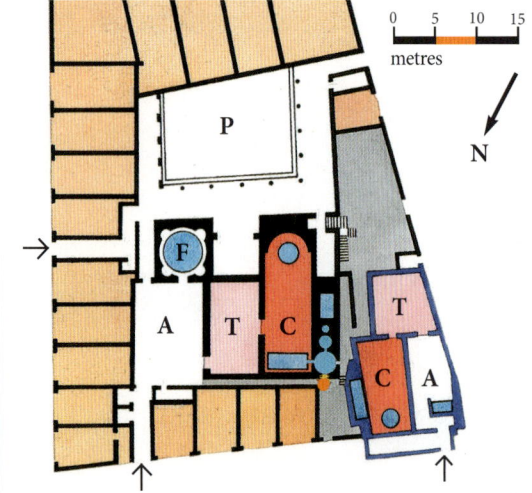

The men's section is outlined in black and the women's in blue. See how the hottest rooms (red) in both suites are arranged on either side of the one furnace (marked by an orange dot).

The blue circles near the furnace are boilers. After losing some heat to the hot rooms, the hot air goes on to warm the warm rooms (pink).

Key:
P: palaestra   T: tepidarium   F: frigidarium
A: apodyterium   C: caldarium

The small arrows mark public entrances.
The orange spaces are shops.

Traditionally it has been thought that everyone went through a set routine of exercise followed by hot and then cold baths, but there is little evidence for this. People may all have done the same things, or they may have had personal preferences as to how they used the facilities.

The entrance hall with the apodyterium beyond (Stabian Baths, Pompeii).

> **Thinking point 2:** Imagine a historian in the future wishes to write about how we use a modern swimming pool or gym. Do you think this would be a difficult or an easy task for them? What kind of evidence might they be able to use? What would they not be able to tell?

The tepidarium: like the apodyterium this sometimes had recesses for clothes (Stabian Baths, Pompeii).

The hot tub in the women's caldarium (Herculaneum).

Around about the middle of the afternoon, I make my way to the public baths just north of the forum. I pay a small admission fee to the doorkeeper and then head to the **palaestra** (exercise area). This is an open space surrounded by a colonnade, rather like a large peristylium. I spend a little time greeting my friends and taking part in some popular exercises, such as throwing and catching a large ball, wrestling and fencing with wooden swords; nothing too serious.

From the palaestra, we walk along a passage into a large hall known as the **apodytērium**. Here we undress, and an enslaved attendant puts our clothes away on shelves along the walls.

Leaving the apodyterium, we pass through an arched doorway into the **tepidārium** (warm room) and spend a little time sitting on benches round the wall in a warm, steamy atmosphere. This prepares us for the higher temperatures in the **caldārium** (hot room). In the caldarium we relax in the large rectangular marble bath filled with hot water, which stretches across the full width of one end of the room.

The caldarium showing a marble bench for sitting or massage (Herculaneum).

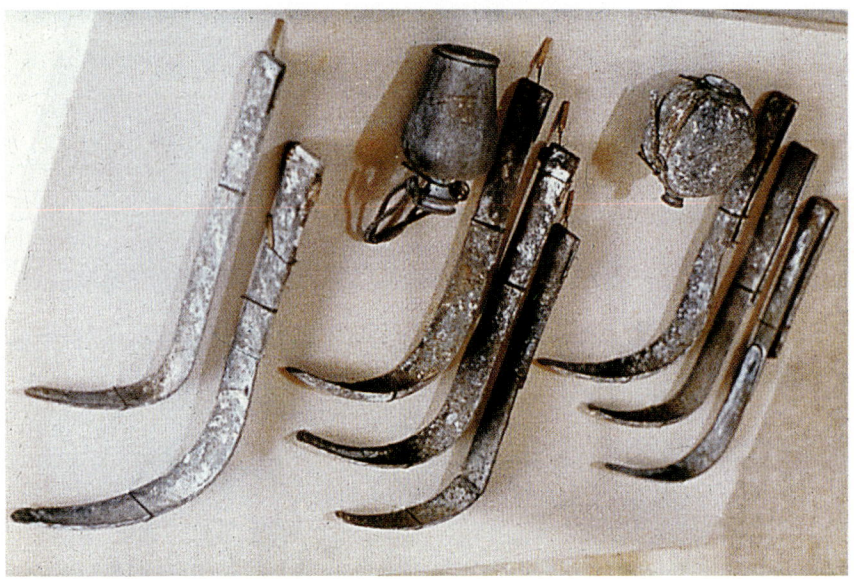

Strigils and oil bottles.

After soaking in the hot bath, I summon an enslaved man to rub me down with olive oil (I bring this with me in a little pot). I lie on a marble slab while he works the oil into my skin before gently removing it and the dirt with a blunt metal scraper known as a **strigil**. I then have a massage and finish by rinsing myself with cold water from the large stone basin at the other end of the caldarium. Before dressing I sometimes visit the **frigidārium** (cold room) and take a plunge in a deep circular pool of unheated water, followed by a brisk rub down with my towel.

Thinking point 3: Create a flow diagram to show Caecilius' routine on one of his visits to the baths. Do we do anything similar in modern gyms or leisure centres?

I also enjoy a visit to the baths. Not all baths have a separate suite of rooms for the use of female bathers, although two here in Pompeii do. Others give access to men and women at different times. Some places allow mixed bathing, but I wouldn't bathe in such a place!

Both the Forum and Stabian Baths had separate facilities for men and women; those for the women are smaller and had a pool of cold water in the apodyterium rather than a separate frigidarium. The smaller facilities may be an indication that fewer women attended the baths, or that women attended less regularly than men. Alternatively, it may indicate that women's needs were regarded as less important than those of men. Some Roman authors mention places that allowed mixed bathing, but it seems to have been considered rather inappropriate. Although Roman women were encouraged to exercise and keep healthy, we do not know whether they were allowed to do so in the palaestra.

Thinking point 4: Why is it so difficult to know for sure why the women's baths were smaller? Have we encountered similar issues anywhere else?

The apodyterium of the women's baths in Herculaneum. What do you think the shelves on the walls were used for?

The baths played an important role in Roman public health along with the sewers, aqueducts and public fountains you learnt about in Stage 3. The water in the baths was nowhere near as hygienic as a modern swimming pool, though. The poet Martial complains about people going to the toilet in the baths and a doctor, Celsus, warned of not going to the baths with an open wound in case it got dirty in the waters and became inflamed.

The Roman writer Seneca gives us a vivid impression of the atmosphere in a bath house:

'I am surrounded by uproar. I live over a set of baths. Just imagine the din that assaults my ears. When the athletic gentlemen below are exercising themselves, lifting lead weights, I can hear their grunts. I can hear the whistling of their breath as it escapes from their lungs. I can hear somebody enjoying a cheap rub down and the smack of the masseur's hands on his shoulders. If his hand comes down flat, it makes one sound; if it comes down hollowed, it makes another. Add to this the noise of a brawler or thief being arrested down below, the racket made by the man who likes to sing in his bath, or the sound of enthusiasts who hurl themselves into the water with a tremendous splash. Next, I can hear the screech of the hair-plucker, who advertises himself by shouting. He is never quiet except when he is plucking hair and making his victim shout instead. Finally, just imagine the cries of the cake seller, the sausage man, and the other food sellers as they advertise their goods round the bath, all adding to the din.'

(Letters to Lucilius/Letter 56)

A bronze statue of a boxer from a set of baths in Rome. His training would no doubt have contributed to the din about which Seneca complains.

Thinking point 5: What three words would you use to characterise the scene described by Seneca? Do you think a trip to the baths would be an enjoyable experience? Why?

Heating the baths

The Romans were not the first people to build public baths (this was one of the many things they learned from the Greeks), but they greatly improved the methods of heating them. Previously water was heated in tanks over a furnace and wood-burners stood in the tepidarium and the caldarium to keep up the air temperature, although they failed to heat the floor.

In the first century BC, the Romans invented the first central heating system. A furnace (usually wood-burning) was placed below the floor level; the floor was supported on small brick piles leaving space through which hot air from the furnace could circulate, warming the floor from below. The hot bath was placed near the furnace, and a steady temperature was maintained by the hot air passing immediately below. Later, channels were built into the walls and warm air from beneath the floor was drawn up through them. This ingenious heating system was known as a **hypocaust**. It was used not only in baths but also in private houses, particularly in the colder parts of the Roman Empire. Many examples have been found in Britain.

A hypocaust viewed from the side.

Hypocaust in the Stabian Baths. Notice the floor suspended on brick piles, so that hot air can circulate beneath and warm both the room and the tank of water for bathing.

Enquiry: How much do we know about a typical visit to a Roman bath house?

You may wish to consider the following:

- what you can and cannot infer from the evidence encountered in this Stage
- the different types of people who would have attended the baths and how much we know about them
- the level of confidence we can have in our claims and why.

Vocabulary checklist 9

agnōscit: agnōvit	*recognises*	**iterum**	*again*
celeriter	*quickly*	**manet: mānsit**	*remains, stays*
cupit: cupīvit	*wants*	**medius**	*middle*
dat: dedit	*gives*	**mox**	*soon*
diēs	*day*	**offert: obtulit**	*offers*
ēmittit: ēmīsit	*throws, sends out*	**ostendit: ostendit**	*shows*
fert: tulit	*brings, carries*	**post**	*after, behind*
homō	*human being, man*	**prōcēdit: prōcessit**	*proceeds, advances*
hospes	*guest*	**pulcher**	*beautiful*
ille	*that*	**revenit: revēnit**	*comes back, returns*
īnspicit: īnspexit	*examines, inspects*	**trādit: trādidit**	*hands over*

The floors of the baths often had marine themes. This mosaic of an octopus was found in the women's baths at Herculaneum.

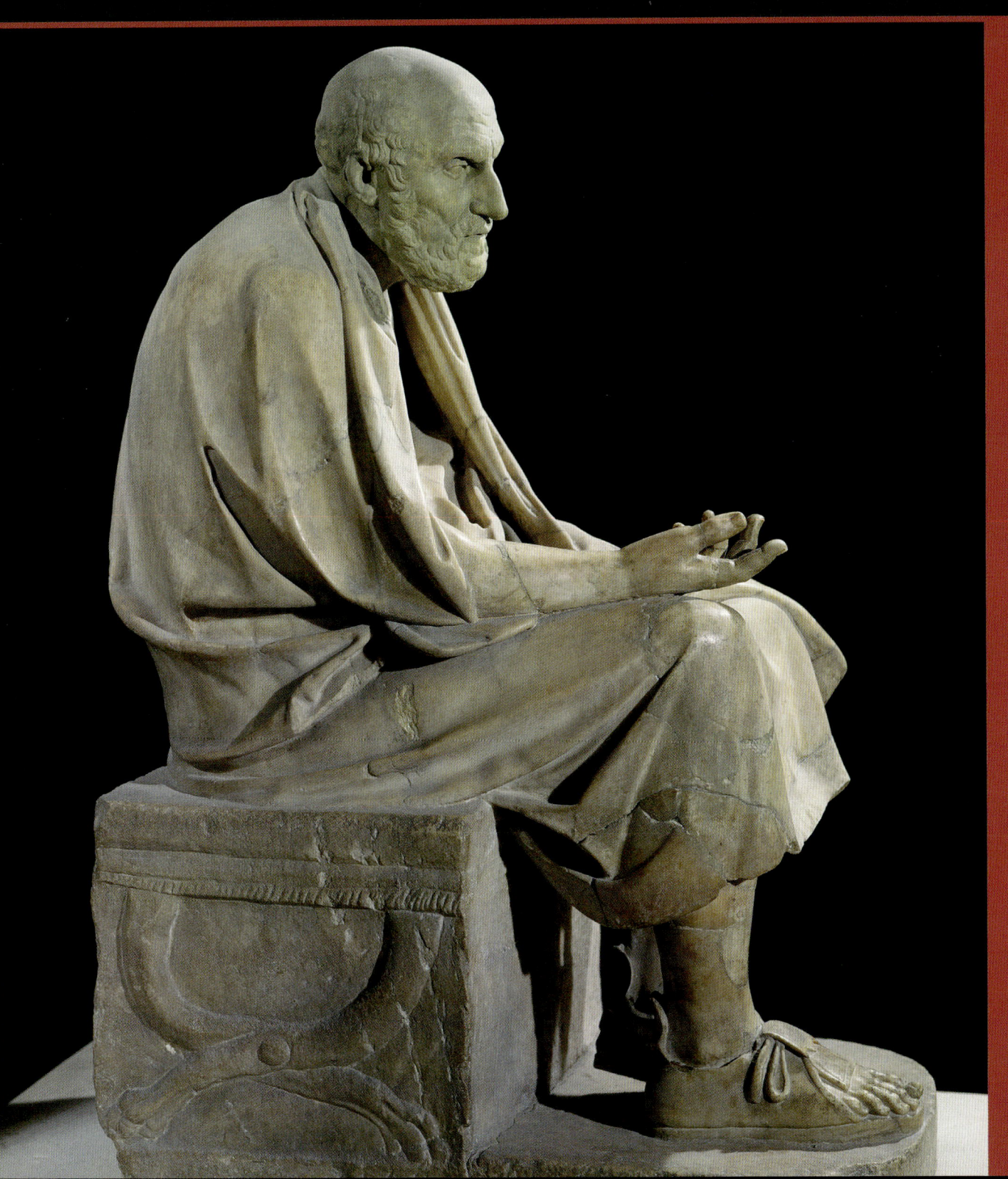

1 Rōmānus dīcit,
'nōs Rōmānī sumus architectī.
nōs viās et pontēs aedificāmus.'

2 'nōs Rōmānī sumus agricolae.
nōs fundōs optimōs habēmus.'

3 Graecus dīcit,
'nōs Graecī sumus sculptōrēs.
nōs statuās pulchrās facimus.'

4 'nōs Graecī sumus artificēs.
nōs pictūrās pingimus.'

5 Rōmānus dīcit,
'vōs Graecī estis ignāvī.
vōs āctōrēs semper spectātis.'

6 Graecus dīcit,
'vōs Rōmānī estis barbarī.
vōs semper pugnātis.'

7 Rōmānus dīcit,
'nōs sumus callidī.
nōs rēs ūtilēs facimus.'

8 Graecus dīcit,
'nōs sumus callidiōrēs quam vōs.
nōs Graecī Rōmānōs docēmus.'

contrōversia

Quīntus amīcum Graecum habēbat. amīcus erat Alexander.
Quīntus et Alexander ad palaestram ībant, ubi rhētor
Graecus erat. hic rhētor erat Theodōrus et prope palaestram
habitābat. in palaestrā erat porticus longa, ubi Theodōrus
iuvenēs docēbat.

    postquam ad hanc porticum vēnērunt, Alexander et
Quīntus rhētorem audīvērunt. rhētor iuvenibus contrōversiam
nūntiābat, 'Graecī sunt meliōrēs quam Rōmānī.'

    Quīntus vehementer exclāmāvit,

    'minimē! nōs Rōmānī sumus meliōrēs quam Graecī.'

    Theodōrus, postquam hanc sententiam audīvit,
respondit,

    'haec est tua sententia. nōs tamen nōn sententiam
quaerimus, nōs argūmentum quaerimus.' tum Quīntus
rhētorī et amīcīs argūmentum explicāvit.

    'nōs Rōmānī sumus fortissimī. nōs barbarōs ferōcissimōs
superāmus. nōs maximum imperium habēmus. nōs pācem
servāmus. vōs Graecī semper contentiōnēs habētis. vōs
semper estis turbulentī.

    'nōs sumus architectī optimī. nōs viās et pontēs ubīque
aedificāmus. urbs Rōma est maior quam omnēs urbēs.

    'postrēmō nōs Rōmānī dīligenter labōrāmus. deī igitur
nōbīs maximum imperium dant. vōs Graecī estis ignāvī. vōs
numquam labōrātis. deī vōbīs nihil dant.'

postquam Quīntus hanc sententiam explicāvit, iuvenēs 25
Pompēiānī vehementer plausērunt et eum laudāvērunt.
deinde Alexander surrēxit. iuvenēs Pompēiānī tacuērunt et
Alexandrum intentē spectāvērunt.

'vōs Rōmānī estis miserandī. vōs maximum imperium
habētis, sed vōs estis imitātōrēs; nōs Graecī sumus 30
auctōrēs. vōs Graecās statuās spectātis, vōs Graecōs librōs
legitis, Graecōs rhētorēs audītis. vōs Rōmānī estis rīdiculī,
quod estis Graeciōrēs quam nōs Graecī!'

iuvenēs, postquam Alexander sententiam suam
explicāvit, rīsērunt. tum Theodōrus nūntiāvit, 35
'Alexander victor est. argūmentum optimum explicāvit.'

deinde	*then*
surrēxit	*got up*
tacuērunt	*fell silent*
miserandī	*pitiful, pathetic*
imitātōrēs	*imitators*
auctōrēs	*creators*
librōs	*books*
rīsērunt	*laughed*

The Romans built this bridge at Alcántara in Spain.

Greek writers and thinkers are still influential today. Here are two
examples: the tragic dramatist Euripides (left) and the philosopher
Anaximander (right). Anaximander is holding a sundial, which he is said
to have invented.

About the language 1

1 In this Stage, you have met sentences with 'we' and 'you':

nōs labōrāmus.	*We work.*	vōs labōrātis.	*You work.*
nōs currimus.	*We run.*	vōs curritis.	*You run.*

Notice that **vōs labōrātis** and **vōs curritis** are **plural** forms. They are used when 'you' refers to more than one person.

2 You have now met the whole of the present tense:

(ego)	portō	*I carry, I am carrying*
(tū)	portās	*you (singular) carry, you are carrying*
	portat	*s/he* carries, s/he* is carrying*
(nōs)	portāmus	*we carry, we are carrying*
(vōs)	portātis	*you (plural) carry, you are carrying*
	portant	*they carry, they are carrying*

* 'it' and 'they' (singular) are also possible for any 's/he' form of the verb.

3 Notice that **nōs** and **vōs** are not strictly necessary, since the endings **-mus** and **-tis** make it clear that 'we' and 'you' are being spoken about. The Romans generally used **nōs** and **vōs** only for emphasis.

4 Further examples:

    a nōs pugnāmus. vōs dormītis.   **c** ambulāmus. dīcimus. vidēmus.

    b vōs clāmātis. nōs audīmus.   **d** vidētis. nūntiātis. intrāmus.

5 The Latin for 'we are' and 'you (plural) are' is as follows:

nōs sumus iuvenēs.	**We are** *young people.*	**vōs estis** artificēs.	**You are** *painters.*
nōs sumus fortēs.	**We are** *brave.*	**vōs estis** ignāvī.	**You are** *lazy.*

So the complete present tense of sum is:

(ego)	sum	*I am*
(tū)	es	*you (singular) are*
	est	*s/he* is*
(nōs)	sumus	*we are*
(vōs)	estis	*you (plural) are*
	sunt	*they are*

* 'it' and 'they' (singular) are also possible for any 's/he' form of the verb.

statuae

Alexander Quīntum ad vīllam dūxit, ubi Alexander et duo
frātrēs habitābant. Alexander frātribus dōnum ferēbat,
quod diem nātālem celebrābant.

'Alexander, quid portās?' rogāvit Quīntus.

'optimās statuās habeō,' respondit amīcus. Alexander
Quīntō duās parvās statuās ostendit. statuae erant senex et
iuvenis.

duo frātrēs in hortō sedēbant. Diodōrus pictūram
pingēbat, Thrasymachus librum Graecum legēbat.
postquam Alexander et Quīntus vīllam intrāvērunt, puerī
ad eōs cucurrērunt.

'vōs estis fēlīcēs,' inquit Alexander. 'ego vōbīs dōnum
habeō quod vōs diem nātālem celebrātis. ecce!' Alexander
frātribus statuās ostendit.

'quam pulcher est iuvenis!' inquit Diodōrus. 'dā mihi eum!'

'minimē! frāter, dā mihi iuvenem!' clāmāvit Thrasymachus.

puerī dissentiēbant et lacrimābant.

'hercle! vōs estis stultissimī puerī!' clāmāvit Alexander
īrātus. 'semper dissentītis, semper lacrimātis. abīte! statuās
retineō!'

puerī, postquam Alexander hoc dīxit, abiērunt. Diodōrus
pictūram in terram dēiēcit, quod īrātus erat. Thrasymachus
librum in piscīnam dēiēcit, quod īrātissimus erat.

tum Quīntus dīxit,

'Alexander, dā mihi statuās! Thrasymache! Diodōre!
venīte hūc! Thrasymache, ecce! ego tibi senem dō, quod
senex erat philosophus. Diodōre, tibi iuvenem dō, quod
iuvenis erat artifex. vōs estis contentī?'

'sumus contentī,' respondērunt puerī.

'ecce, Alexander,' inquit Quīntus, 'vōs Graeculī estis
optimī artificēs sed turbulentī. nōs Rōmānī vōbīs pācem
damus.'

Diodōrus ad Quīntum cucurrit. puer Quīntō pictūram
dedit.

'et vōs praemium accipitis,' susurrāvit Thrasymachus.

frātrēs *brothers*

ad eōs cucurrērunt
  ran towards them
fēlīcēs *lucky, fortunate*

quam pulcher *how handsome*
dā! *give!*
dissentiēbant
  began to argue
abīte! *go away!*
retineō *am keeping*
abiērunt *went away*
in terram dēiēcit
  threw onto the ground
in piscīnam *into the fish pond*

venīte hūc! *come here!*
philosophus *philosopher*
praemium *reward, prize*
susurrāvit
  whispered, muttered

statuae.

About the language 2

1 Study the following pairs of sentences:

nōs Rōmānī sumus callidī.
We Romans are clever.

nōs Rōmānī sumus **callidiōrēs** quam vōs Graecī.
*We Romans are **cleverer** than you Greeks.*

nōs Rōmānī sumus fortēs.
We Romans are brave.

nōs Rōmānī sumus **fortiōrēs** quam vōs Graecī.
*We Romans are **braver** than you Greeks.*

The words in **bold** are known as **comparatives**. They are used to compare
two things or groups with each other. In the examples above, the Romans
are comparing themselves with the Greeks.

2 Further examples:

   a Pompēiānī sunt stultī. Nūcerīnī sunt stultiōrēs quam Pompēiānī.

   b Diodōrus erat īrātus, sed Thrasymachus erat īrātior quam Diodōrus.

   c mea vīlla est pulchra, sed tua vīlla est pulchrior quam mea.

3 The word **magnus** forms its comparative in an unusual way:

Nūceria est magna.   Rōma est maior quam Nūceria.
Nuceria is large.   *Rome is larger than Nuceria.*

Roman writing materials.

Lūcia et Alexander

Lūcia et Melissa prope palaestram ambulant. Lūcia Alexandrum videt.

Lūcia:	Melissa, ecce! iuvenis ille est Alexander.
Melissa:	quis est Alexander?
Lūcia:	Alexander est iuvenis Graecus. Theodōrus in palaestrā cotīdiē Alexandrum et Quīntum docet. Quīntus et Alexander amīcissimī sunt.
Melissa:	quam pulcher est Alexander!
Lūcia:	Alexander est callidissimus. herī Alexander rhētorī et amīcīs optimum argūmentum explicāvit.
Melissa:	Quīntus quoque callidus est.
Lūcia:	Alexander est callidior quam Quīntus. nōs Rōmānī nōn semper sumus meliōrēs quam Graecī.
Melissa:	Alexander tē dēlectat, Lūcia?
Lūcia:	minimē! quam rīdicula es, Melissa!
	(Lūcia ērubēscit.)

5

10

15

amīcissimī
   very friendly, very good friends
callidissimus *very clever*

callidior *more clever*

ērubēscit *blushes*

Practising the language

ānulus Aegyptius

The owners of a ring all experience bad luck.

Syphāx in tabernā sedēbat. caupō Syphācī vīnum dedit. Syphāx caupōnī ānulum trādidit.

'pecūniam nōn habeō,' inquit, 'quod Neptūnus nāvem meam dēlēvit.'

caupō, postquam ānulum accēpit, eum īnspiciēbat. 5

'ānulus antīquus est,' inquit Syphāx. 'servus Aegyptius mihi ānulum dedit. servus in pȳramide ānulum invēnit.'

caupō uxōrī ānulum ostendit. caupō uxōrī ānulum dedit, quod ānulus eam dēlectāvit. 10

uxor postrīdiē ambulābat. subitō fūr in viā appāruit. pecūniam postulāvit. fēmina, quod erat perterrita, fūrī pecūniam dedit. fūr ānulum cōnspexit. ānulum postulāvit. fēmina fūrī eum trādidit.

fēmina ad tabernam rediit et marītum invēnit. caupō 15 incendium spectābat. ēheu! taberna ardēbat! fēmina marītō rem tōtam nārrāvit.

'ānulus īnfēlīx est,' inquit caupō. 'ānulus tabernam dēlēvit.'

fur, postquam pecūniam et ānulum cēpit, trēs 20 inimīcōs cōnspexit. inimīcī, postquam pecūniam cōnspexērunt, fūrem verberābant. fūr fūgit, sed ānulum āmīsit.

Grumiō cum Poppaeā ambulābat. ānulum in viā invēnit. coquus Poppaeae ānulum dedit. 25

'ānulus Aegyptius est,' inquit. 'euge! ānulus fēlīx est.'

Aegyptius *Egyptian*	
caupō *innkeeper*	
Neptūnus *Neptune (god of the sea)*	
dēlēvit *has destroyed*	
eum *it*	
antīquus *old, ancient*	
in pȳramide *in a pyramid*	
eam *her*	
postrīdiē *on the next day*	
marītum *husband*	
incendium *blaze, fire*	
ardēbat *was on fire*	
īnfēlīx *unlucky*	
inimīcōs *enemies*	
āmīsit *lost*	

Bronze ring with the heads of Egyptian gods.

1 Explore the story

a 'pecūniam nōn habeō,' inquit, 'quod Neptūnus nāvem meam dēlēvit' (lines 3–4): what reason did Syphax give for not having any money to pay with?

b 'ānulus antīquus est,' inquit Syphāx. 'servus Aegyptius mihi ānulum dedit. servus in pȳramide ānulum invēnit' (lines 6–8): what three things did Syphax say about the ring?

c caupō uxōrī ānulum ostendit. caupō uxōrī ānulum dedit, quod ānulus eam dēlectāvit (lines 9–10): what two things did the innkeeper do with the ring?

d uxor postrīdiē ambulābat. subitō fūr in viā appāruit (line 11): write down the Latin word that indicates who the innkeeper's wife met in the street?

e pecūniam postulāvit. fēmina, quod erat perterrita, fūrī pecūniam dedit. fūr ānulum cōnspexit. ānulum postulāvit. fēmina fūrī eum trādidit (lines 12–14): what two things did the woman have to give up?

f fēmina ad tabernam rediit et marītum invēnit. caupō incendium spectābat. ēheu! taberna ardēbat! (lines 15–16): when the woman returned to the inn what did she discover was happening to it?

g inimīcī, postquam pecūniam cōnspexērunt, fūrem verberābant. fūr fūgit, sed ānulum āmīsit (lines 21–23): what three things happened after the thief's enemies saw the money?

h Grumiō cum Poppaeā ambulābat. ānulum in viā invēnit (line 24–25): who found the ring?

i coquus Poppaeae ānulum dedit (line 25): what did the cook do with the ring?

2 Explore the language

Explain why **caupō** (line 1) and **caupōnī** (line 2) have different endings.

dative: page 144

3 Explore further

Look at line 26 ('**ānulus Aegyptius est,**' inquit. '**euge! ānulus fēlīx est.**').

Do you agree with Grumio's conclusion?

Reviewing the language Stage 10: page 232

Enquiry: How did the Roman education system prepare Roman children for adult life?

Schools

The first stage of education

There was no law which forced parents to send their children to school, and those who wanted education for their children had to pay for it. The advantages of being able to read and write were so widely appreciated, though, that many people were prepared to pay the relatively small fee for their sons, and perhaps their daughters too, to go to school for at least a few years.

Quintus, and perhaps Lucia, would first have gone to school when they were about 7 years old. This school would have been small, consisting of about thirty pupils and a teacher known as the **lūdī magister**. All the teaching would take place in a rented room or perhaps in a public colonnade or square.

Thinking point 1: Consider the stories in this Stage. What do you already know about Quintus' experience of school? How does it differ from yours?

The first school I attended was held in a public square; it was sometimes hard to concentrate with all the noise and distractions. I did my best to pay attention, though, as the teacher was very strict and I didn't want to be punished!

The school day began early and lasted for six hours with a short break at midday. On the walk to and from school I was escorted by an enslaved man known as a **paedagōgus**, who was responsible for making sure I behaved properly and stayed safe. Another enslaved man carried my books and writing materials.

There are no lessons during public festivals and market days. Also during the hot summer months fewer pupils attend lessons, so some teachers close their schools altogether from July to October.

At the school of the ludi magister, I learned to read and write Latin and Greek and do simple arithmetic. Both Lucia and I could already speak some Greek before we began school; we picked it up from enslaved Greeks at home and from friends like Alexander.

There were generally no desks and no board for the teacher to write on. Pupils sat on benches or stools, resting tablets on their knees. The teacher sat on a high chair overlooking his class.

Stone relief of a school lesson from the second century AD, found near Trier in Germany.

Thinking point 2: Look at this relief. Which figures do you think represent the teacher and the two students? Who might the fourth figure be? Give reasons for your claims.

Writing materials

Usually we write on **tabulae** (wooden tablets) coated with a thin film of wax. Several tablets can be strung together to make a little writing book. We write the letters on the wax surface with a **stilus** (a thin stick made of metal, bone or ivory). The end opposite the writing point is flat, so you can use it to rub out mistakes and make the wax smooth again; Lucia teases me that I need that end of the stilus more often than the sharp end!

A wax tablet with a student's exercise in Greek: the teacher has written the top two lines and the student has copied them below.

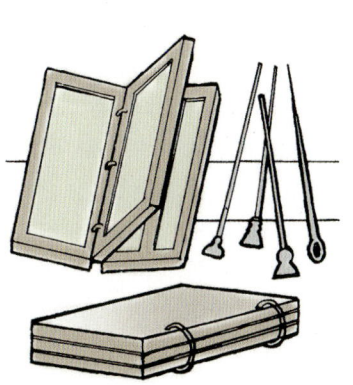

tabulae and stili.

Thinking point 3: Look carefully at the photograph of a wax tablet. How can you tell that the top two lines were written by the teacher and the bottom were done by the student?

Sometimes students wrote with ink on papyrus, a material that looked rather like modern paper but was rougher in texture. It was manufactured from the fibres of the papyrus reed that grew along the banks of the river Nile in Egypt. For writing on papyrus they used either a reed or a goose quill sharpened and split at one end like a fountain pen nib.

Ink was made from soot (black powder produced when things like coal and wood are burned) and a gummy substance such as resin extracted from plants. These were used to form a paste that was thinned by adding water. The best inks were so hard and durable that the writing on some pieces of papyrus is still perfectly legible today.

Papyrus rolls, a double inkwell (for red and black ink) and a quill pen. Copied from a Pompeian painting.

The second stage

Many children would have finished their schooling at the age of eleven, but a boy like Quintus from a wealthy family would have moved to a more advanced school run by a **grammaticus**.

The grammaticus introduced me to the work of important Greek and Roman writers, beginning with the Iliad and Odyssey of Homer. I preferred the Odyssey; I love the idea of travelling the world and having adventures! Then we moved on to the famous Greek tragedies. In terms of Latin literature almost everyone studies the works of Virgil and Horace. We were also taught a little history and geography, but this was mainly to understand references to famous people and places in literature.

We read these works of literature aloud, analysed the grammar and learned long passages by heart. Father says that being able to quote or recite these passages in adulthood is a sign of being well educated and will help me to make a good impression on people. I still find it boring, though! I'd much rather enjoy reading literature than spend ages memorising it.

When he left the grammaticus at the age of 15 or 16, Quintus would have had a very good knowledge of Greek as well as Latin. A knowledge of Greek introduced pupils to a culture which had a great deal of influence on the Romans and was also very useful, as Greek was widely spoken in the countries of the eastern Mediterranean where Roman merchants and government officials frequently travelled on business.

Thinking point 4: Which authors or works are almost always studied in school today? Why do you think certain works are considered so important?

This roughly sketched painting shows a school in session in the colonnade of the forum at Pompeii. On the right a boy is supported on another's back for a beating; he is probably being punished for misbehaviour or poor performance.

The third stage

A few students then proceeded to the school of a **rhētor** like Theodorus in our story. This teacher, who was often a highly educated Greek, gave more advanced lessons in literature and trained students in the art of public speaking.

Public speaking is a very important skill to learn if I want to take part in public life one day; I might need it to present cases in the law courts, to express my opinions in council meetings, or even to address the people at election time if I want to get into politics!

Theodorus teaches us the rules for making different kinds of speeches and makes us practise arguing for and against a point of view. We also learn how to vary our tone of voice and emphasise our words with gestures.

Thinking point 5: Do you learn public speaking or debating skills in your school? Do you think they are still important today?

Scientific and technical subjects

The Greeks made important discoveries in mathematics and some aspects of physics, and the Romans were experienced in the methods of surveying and the use of concrete in building, but school work had little to do with such things. Roman schools taught the ability to read and write, a knowledge of simple arithmetic, the appreciation of fine literature, and the ability to speak and argue convincingly, all thought to be essential for someone to be considered well educated. Scientific thinking and advanced mathematics were taught to only a few students whose parents were interested and wealthy enough to pay the fees of a specialist teacher, who was nearly always Greek. Technical skills were learnt by becoming an apprentice in a trade or business.

> **Thinking point 6:** Think about the subjects that you study or might be able to study in the future. How are these different from what was on offer for young Romans? Compare the goals of education for the Romans and the goals of education today.

Craft skills were learned by apprenticeship. Here we see some men carving a table leg.

Girls' education

Some girls go to the school of the ludi magister, but many girls pick up knowledge of reading and writing from their parents or brothers at home. Some wealthy families have an enslaved private tutor as part of their household or they hire one to teach their daughters things like music, Latin and Greek literature, and philosophy. The hope is that if a girl is well educated she'll attract a good husband, but personally I just enjoy studying.

Girls are expected to learn skills which will be useful in their future married life. For example, I need to be good at basic arithmetic, as I'll be expected to keep track of the household finances. Daughters in poorer households may learn a trade like spinning or weaving, so that they can contribute to the household income. They also learn skills such as cooking, cleaning and childcare, but I will have enslaved people in my household to do these things for me.

Thinking point 7: In the modern world, is the education of boys still viewed differently to that of girls? Do boys and girls study different things? Compare the ideas of different places and cultures.

Thinking point 8: Think back over the information you've read in this Stage. What role did enslaved people play in the education of Roman children?

Enquiry: How did the Roman education system prepare Roman children for adult life?

You may wish to consider the following:

- the three stages of education; the material taught and their purposes
- how the education of boys compared with that of girls
- how the education of poorer children compared with that of the wealthier.

Vocabulary checklist 10

abit: abiit	*goes away*	**nūntiat: nūntiāvit**	*announces*
accipit: accēpit	*accepts*	**pāx**	*peace*
callidus	*clever*	**portus**	*harbour*
capit: cēpit	*captures, takes*	**quam**	*than; how*
contentus	*satisfied*	**semper**	*always*
exclāmat: exclāmāvit	*exclaims*	**servat: servāvit**	*saves, keeps (safe)*
frāter	*brother*	**sōlus**	*alone, lonely*
habitat: habitāvit	*lives*	**suus**	*his, her, their*
imperium	*empire*	**tacet: tacuit**	*is silent, is quiet*
invenit: invēnit	*finds*	**uxor**	*wife*
liber	*book*	**vehementer**	*loudly, energetically*
nōs	*we*	**vōs**	*you (plural)*

Painting found in Pompeii depicting a woman holding wax tablets and a stylus.

1 cīvēs in forō candidātōs spectant.

2 agricolae clāmant,
  'nōs candidātum optimum habēmus.'
  'candidātus noster est Lūcius.'
  'nōs Lūciō favēmus.'

3 mercātōrēs agricolīs respondent,
  'nōs candidātum optimum habēmus.'
  'candidātus noster est mercātor.'
  'nōs mercātōrī favēmus.'

4 pistōrēs in forō clāmant,
  'nōs pistōrēs candidātum optimum habēmus.'
  'candidātus noster est pistor.'
  'nōs pistōrī crēdimus.'

5 iuvenēs pistōribus respondent,
  'nōs iuvenēs candidātum optimum habēmus.'
  'candidātus noster est āthlēta.'
  'nōs āthlētae crēdimus.'

6 fūrēs clāmant,
  'nōs quoque candidātum habēmus.'
  'candidātus noster est fūr.'
  'nōs candidātō nostrō nōn crēdimus sed favēmus.'

titulī

titulī *notices, slogans*

in hortō

Caecilius cum Quīntō per hortum ambulābat. Lūcia quoque
erat in hortō. Caecilius fīliō dīxit,

'Holcōnius candidātus optimus est. Holcōnius est vir nōbilis.
Pompēiānī Holcōniō crēdunt, quod pater senātor erat.'

Lūcia, postquam patrem audīvit, sibi dīxit,

'sed Āfer candidātus līberālis est. Āfer cīvibus Pompēiānīs
spectāculum splendidum in amphitheātrō prōmīsit.'

candidātus *candidate*
vir nōbilis *man of noble birth*
5 **crēdunt** *believe in, trust*
sibi dīxit *said to herself*
līberālis *generous*
prōmīsit *has promised*

prope vīllam I

nox erat. Quīntus et Clēmēns ad vīllam reveniēbant. parvam
tabernam cōnspexērunt, ubi scrīptor labōrābat. scrīptor
Sulla erat. Sulla hunc titulum in mūrō scrībēbat:

'caupōnēs Āfrō crēdunt.'

Quīntus, postquam titulum cōnspexit, erat īrātus. Quīntus
scrīptōrī dīxit,

'scrīptor! corrige illum titulum! Holcōnius melior est
quam Āfer.'

Clēmēns Sullae decem dēnāriōs dedit. Sulla rīdēbat.
postquam Quīntus et Clēmēns vīllam intrāvērunt, ita
titulum corrēxit:

'caudicēs Āfrō crēdunt.'

scrīptor *signwriter*
in mūrō *on the (outside) wall*

5

corrige! *amend! put right!*

10

corrēxit *amended, put right*
caudicēs *idiots*

prope vīllam II

Lūcia et Melissa ē vīllā māne discēdēbant. Lūcia titulum
novum cōnspexit. postquam titulum lēgit, īrāta erat. Lūcia
Melissae eum ostendit.

    'titulus ille est rīdiculus,' inquit. 'multī Pompēiānī Āfrō
favent. nōn sunt caudicēs.'

    'cōnsilium optimum habeō,' Melissa Lūciae respondit.

    Melissa ad īnsulam festīnāvit, ubi Sulla habitābat. Melissa
īnsulam intrāvit et Sullam excitāvit. Melissa et Sulla ad
parvam tabernam contendērunt, ubi Lūcia manēbat.

    postquam ad tabernam vēnērunt, Lūcia Sullae titulum
ostendit.

    'ērāde illam īnscrīptiōnem!' inquit.

    Melissa scrīptōrī decem dēnāriōs dedit.

    'placetne tibi?' rogāvit.

    'mihi placet,' scrīptor laetus Melissae respondit. nunc
vīgintī dēnāriōs habēbat.

    Sulla, postquam īnscrīptiōnem ērāsit, hunc titulum
scrīpsit:

lēgit *read*

5   **favent** *favour, support*
cōnsilium *plan, idea*
īnsulam *block of flats*

10

ērāde! *remove! erase!*
īnscrīptiōnem *writing*
placetne tibi?
15   *does it please you? does it*
    suit you?
vīgintī *twenty*
ērāsit *removed, erased*
līberālissimī *very generous*

LVCIA ET QVINTVS SVNT LIBERALISSIMI

About the language 1

1 In Stage 9, you met the dative case:

   Quīntus **amīcīs** discum ostendit.
   *Quintus showed the discus **to his friends**.*

   Metella **fīliō** dōnum quaerēbat.
   *Metella was looking for a gift **for her son**.*

dative: page 144

2 In this Stage, you have met some further examples:

   Quīntus **Holcōniō** favet.   nōs **pistōrī** crēdimus.
   *Quintus gives support **to Holconius**.*   *We give our trust **to the baker**.*

3 The sentences above can be translated more simply:

   Quīntus Holcōniō favet.   nōs pistōrī crēdimus.
   Quintus supports Holconius.   *We trust the baker.*

4 Further examples:
   a nōs Āfrō favēmus.
   b vōs amīcīs crēditis.
   c mercātōrēs candidātō nostrō nōn crēdunt.

   Notice the following use of the dative with the verb **placet**:
   placetne tibi?   mihi placet.
   Is it pleasing to you?   *It is pleasing to me.*

   There are more natural ways of translating these examples, such as:
   Does it please you?   *Yes, it pleases me.*
   Do you like it?   *Yes, I do.*

   Notice the dative of **nōs** and **vōs**:
   nōs sumus fortēs. deī **nōbīs** imperium dant.
   *We are brave. The gods give an empire **to us**.*

   vōs estis ignāvī. deī **vōbīs** nihil dant.
   *You are lazy. The gods give nothing **to you**.*

Lūcius Spurius Pompōniānus

in vīllā

Grumiō ē culīnā contendit. Clēmēns Grumiōnem videt.

Clēmēns:	babae! togam splendidam geris!	**babae!** *hey!*
Grumiō:	placetne tibi?	
Clēmēns:	mihi placet. quō festīnās, Grumiō?	**quō** *where?*
Grumiō:	ad amphitheātrum contendō. Āfer fautōrēs	5 **fautōrēs** *supporters*
	exspectat.	
Clēmēns:	num tū Āfrō favēs? Caecilius Holcōniō favet.	
Grumiō:	Āfer fautōribus quīnque dēnāriōs prōmīsit.	**quīnque** *five*
	Holcōnius fautōribus duōs dēnāriōs tantum	**tantum** *only*
	prōmīsit. ego Āfrō faveō, quod vir līberālis est.	10
Clēmēns:	sed tū servus es. cīvis Pompēiānus nōn es. Āfer	
	cīvibus Pompēiānīs pecūniam prōmīsit.	
Grumiō:	Clēmēns, hodiē nōn sum Grumiō. hodiē sum	
	Lūcius Spurius Pompōniānus!	
Clēmēns:	Lūcius Spurius Pompōniānus! mendācissimus	15 **mendācissimus**
	coquus es!	*very deceitful*
Grumiō:	minimē! hodiē sum pistor Pompēiānus. hodiē	
	nōs pistōrēs ad amphitheātrum convenīmus.	**ad amphitheātrum**
	nōs Āfrum ad forum dūcimus, ubi cīvēs	**convenīmus**
	ōrātiōnēs exspectant. ego ad amphitheātrum	20 *are meeting at the*
	contendō. tū mēcum venīs?	*amphitheatre*
Clēmēns:	tēcum veniō. Āfrō nōn faveō. dēnāriōs nōn cupiō,	**ōrātiōnēs** *speeches*
	sed dē tē sollicitus sum. rem perīculōsam suscipis.	**mēcum** *with me*
	(exeunt.)	**tēcum** *with you*
		dē tē *about you*
		perīculōsam *dangerous*
		suscipis *you are taking on*
		exeunt *they go out*

This notice reads:
'Vote for Cnaeus Helvius
Sabinus as aedile. He
deserves public office.'

prope amphitheātrum

multī pistōrēs ad amphitheātrum conveniunt. Grumiō et Clēmēns ad hanc turbam festīnant.

dīvīsor:	festīnāte! festīnāte! nōs Āfrum exspectāmus.
Grumiō:	salvē, dīvīsor! ego sum Lūcius Spurius Pompōniānus et hic *(Grumiō Clēmentem pulsat)* servus meus est. ego et Āfer amīcissimī sumus.
dīvīsor:	ecce quīnque dēnāriī!
	(dīvīsor Grumiōnī dēnāriōs dat. dīvīsor Grumiōnī fūstem quoque trādit.)
Grumiō:	Āfer mihi dēnāriōs, nōn fūstem prōmīsit.
Clēmēns:	Āfer vir līberālis est.
Grumiō:	tacē, pessime serve!
dīvīsor:	fūstēs ūtilissimī sunt. Holcōnius et amīcī sunt in forō.
pistor:	ecce Āfer! Āfer adest!
	(Āfer et fautōrēs per viās ad forum contendunt.)

festīnāte! *hurry!*

dīvīsor *divisor (agent hired to distribute bribes)*

5

10

tacē! *be quiet!*

ūtilissimī *very useful*

15

Pompeians listening to a candidate speaking from the steps of the Temple of Jupiter, Juno and Minerva (the Capitoline Triad) in the forum.

in forō

pistōrēs cum Clēmente et cum Grumiōne Āfrum ad forum dūcunt.

pistor prīmus:	Pompēiānī Āfrō favent.	
pistor secundus:	Āfer est melior quam Holcōnius.	
pistor tertius:	nōs Āfrō crēdimus.	5

tertius *third*

Clēmēns:	Grumiō! in forō sunt Holcōnius et amīcī.
	Holcōnium et amīcōs videō.
Grumiō:	euge! fēminās videō, ancillās videō, puellās . . . ēheu! Caecilium videō! Caecilius cum Holcōniō stat! ad vīllam reveniō!

10

Clēmēns:	Grumiō, manē!
	(*Grumiō fugit.*)

manē! *wait! stay here!*

mercātor prīmus:	Holcōnius est vir nōbilis.	
mercātor secundus:	Holcōnius melior est quam Āfer.	15
mercātor tertius:	nōs mercātōrēs Holcōniō favēmus.	
	(*pistōrēs et mercātōrēs conveniunt. īrātī sunt.*)	

pistor prīmus:	Holcōnius est asinus. vōs quoque estis asinī, quod Holcōniō crēditis.	20

asinus *donkey*

mercātor prīmus:	Āfer est caudex. vōs quoque estis caudicēs, quod Āfrō crēditis.
pistor secundus:	amīcī! mercātōrēs nōs 'caudicēs' vocant.

	nōs nōn sumus caudicēs. fortissimī sumus. fūstēs habēmus.	25

mercātor secundus:	amīcī! pistōrēs nōs 'asinōs' vocant. nōs nōn sumus asinī. nōs fortiōrēs sumus quam pistōrēs. magnōs fūstēs habēmus.	30
	(*mercātōrēs et pistōrēs in forō pugnant.*)	

Candidates also made speeches from a special platform in the forum.

in culīnā

Clēmēns in culīnā sedet. Grumiō intrat.

Clēmēns: salvē, Pompōniāne! hercle! toga tua scissa est!   **scissa** *torn*

Grumiō: ēheu! Holcōnius et amīcī in forō mē cēpērunt.
postquam fūstem meum cōnspexērunt,
clāmābant, 'ecce pistor fortis!' tum mercātōrēs   *5*
mē verberāvērunt. dēnāriōs meōs rapuērunt.   **rapuērunt** *seized, grabbed*
nunc nūllōs dēnāriōs habeō.

Clēmēns: ego decem dēnāriōs habeō!

Grumiō: decem dēnāriōs?

Clēmēns: Caecilius mihi decem dēnāriōs dedit, quod   *10*
servus fidēlis sum. postquam pistōrēs et
mercātōrēs pugnam commīsērunt, Caecilius mē   **commīsērunt** *began*
cōnspexit. duo pistōrēs Caecilium verberābant.
dominus noster auxilium postulābat. Caecilius   **noster** *our*
mēcum ē forō effūgit. dominus noster mihi   *15*   **auxilium** *help*
decem dēnāriōs dedit, quod līberālis est.   **effūgit** *escaped*

Grumiō: Caecilius est . . .

Clēmēns: valē, Pompōniāne!

Grumiō: quō festīnās, Clēmēns?

Clēmēns: ad portum festīnō. ibi Poppaea mē exspectat.   *20*
placetne tibi?

Grumiō: mihi nōn placet!

About the language 2

1 From Stage 1 onwards, you have met phrases of the following kind:

| **in** hortō | **ad** vīllam | **ex** arēnā | **per** viās |
| *in the garden* | *to the house* | *out of the arena* | *through the streets* |

The words in **bold** are **prepositions**.

2 The prepositions **ad**, **per** and **prope** are used with the accusative case:

| **ad** portum | **per** urbem | **prope** puerōs |
| *to the harbour* | *through the town* | *near the boys* |

nominative case and accusative case: page 123

3 The prepositions **cum**, **de**, **ē** and **ex** are used with a different case, known as the ablative:

| **cum** Quīntō | **ē** tabernā | **ex** ātriō | **dē** monte |
| *with Quintus* | *out of the shop* | *out of the atrium* | *down from the mountain* |

4 Further examples:

   a turba ad urbem contendit.

   b hospitēs cum mercātōre cēnābant.

   c Clēmēns dē coquō sollicitus erat.

   d Caecilius et Metella per hortum ambulābant.

   e multae tabernae erant prope thermās.

   f Lūcia et Melissa ē vīllā discessērunt.

5 Notice how the preposition **in** is used:

cīvēs **in forum** cucurrērunt.

*The citizens ran **into the forum**.*

mercātōrēs **in forō** negōtium agēbant.

*The merchants were doing business **in the forum**.*

in meaning *into* or *onto* is used with the accusative.

in meaning *in* or *on* is used with the ablative.

Further examples:

   a Metella hospitēs in trīclīnium dūxit.

   b canis in mēnsam salit.

   c multī spectātōrēs in theātrō sedēbant.

   d āctōrēs in scaenā stābant.

Reviewing the language Stage 11: page 233

Lūcia et Metella

Lūcia et māter sunt in hortō.

Metella:	Lūcia, pater tuus tibi marītum quaerit. Holcōniō igitur epistulam scrīpsit, quod Holcōnius multōs amīcōs habet. hodiē Holcōnius respondit, 'ego amīcum dīvitem et seniōrem habeō. amīcus est

epistulam *letter*

dīvitem *rich*
seniōrem *older*

	Umbricius. uxor est mortua et trēs līberōs habet. uxōrem novam quaerit.' pater igitur tibi Umbricium ēlēgit. epistulam ad eum mīsit. placetne tibi?
Lūcia:	ēheu! mihi nōn placet!

(Lūcia lacrimat.)

Metella:	quid dīcis? cūr lacrimās?
Lūcia:	lacrimō, quod Alexandrum amō. iuvenis callidus et bonus est.

amō *love*
bonus *good, worthy*

Metella:	mea columba! fortasse Alexander est iuvenis callidus et bonus, sed Umbricius est vir nōbilis et līberālis.
Lūcia:	sed Alexander mē dēlectat!

(Lūcia lacrimat et ex hortō currit.)

postrīdiē Metella Lūciam in ātrium vocat. Lūcia est trīstissima.

trīstissima *very sad*

Metella:	pater tuus est īrātissimus. Umbricius epistulam mīsit.
Lūcia:	quid est in epistulā? cūr pater īrātus est?
Metella:	Umbricius uxōrem novam habet! ancillam līberāvit et eam in mātrimōnium dūxit. haec ancilla Umbricium et līberōs diū cūrāvit.

in mātrimōnium dūxit
   has married
diū *for a long time*
cūrāvit *has cared for*
laribus *Lares (household gods)*

Lūcia:	quam fēlīx sum! ego laribus maximās grātiās agō, quod mē servāvērunt.

(Metella exit.)

Lūcia:	*(sollicita)* sed quam īnfēlīx est līberta . . .

līberta *freedwoman*

Local government and elections

Possible meeting place of the town council near the forum.

Thinking point 1: Write a definition of the words 'democracy,' 'empire' and 'election'. What do you think makes a system 'democratic' or not?

The Pompeians take local politics seriously, and the annual elections at the end of March are very lively. People write slogans on the walls, groups of supporters hold processions through the streets and the candidates speak at public meetings in the forum. Public speaking is so important in convincing people to vote for you; this is one reason why it's such a big part of the education of boys like Quintus who might want political careers one day.

Every year, two pairs of officials are elected by the people; well, by the freeborn, male citizens as they are the only people who can vote. The senior pair, called **duovirī** or **duumvirī**, are responsible for hearing evidence and giving judgment in the law court. The other pair, called **aedīlēs**, make sure that the public services are efficiently run and the local taxes are spent wisely. They supervise the public markets, public order, the baths, places of public entertainment, the water supply and the sewers.

In addition to these four elected officials, there is a town council of 100 citizens, most of whom have already served as duoviri or aediles. New members of the council are chosen by the council itself, not by a popular vote.

Thinking point 2: Who does Lucia tell us is able to vote? Who in Pompeii was not able to vote? Which do you think is the larger group?

Only freeborn men who own more than the minimum level of property can stand as candidates; one day Quintus might be able to stand, but I won't. The candidates wear a toga whitened with chalk so that they can be easily recognised. The word **candidātus** comes from **candidus** which means 'dazzling white'.

As the candidates walk around attended by their clients and greeting voters, their agents praise their qualities, make promises on their behalf and distribute money as bribes. This bribery is illegal, but it happens all the time! Promises of games and entertainments are the more legal forms of persuasion. In fact, it's expected that those who get elected will show their gratitude to the voters by paying for and putting on splendid shows in the theatre and amphitheatre.

> **Thinking point 3:** What did candidates do to get more votes? What do you think of this behaviour? Can you think of similarities or differences with modern elections?

A successful candidate would also be expected to pay for the construction or repair of public buildings. The family of the Holconii, whose names often appear in the lists of Pompeian duoviri and aediles, were connected with the building of the large theatre, and another wealthy family, the Flacci, helped to pay for other civic buildings and had a reputation for putting on first-class entertainments.

The tradition of public service made it possible for a small town like Pompeii to enjoy benefits which could not have been paid for by local taxes alone. It also meant that men who wanted to take part in local government had to be wealthy. They came from two groups: a small core of wealthy families, like the Holconii, whose members were regularly elected to the most important offices; and a larger group, the make-up of which changed frequently, who tended to be elected to less powerful positions.

> **Thinking point 4:** Explain how private wealth impacted on who was able to stand for election and how likely someone was to win.

The public officials might offer free bread to the poor. One election slogan recommends a candidate who 'brings good bread'. It has been suggested that this is what is depicted in this wall painting from the House of Julia Felix.

Copies of this inscription were found over both east and west entrances to Pompeii's amphitheatre. It states that the duumvirs Quinctius Valgus and Marcus Porcius paid for the amphitheatre to be built.

Although public service isn't paid, it does give a man a position of importance in the town. There is never a shortage of candidates wanting to compete in elections, hoping to win honour and fame among their fellow citizens. The really good, wide seats in the front row of the theatre – which give a close-up view of the chorus and actors – are reserved for such men, and they also have a special place close to the arena in the amphitheatre. Eventually the town council might erect a statue to them, and if they contribute to the construction or repair of a building they might get their name inscribed on it.

My father hasn't ever really been interested in standing as a candidate. He prefers to concentrate on his business activities and lend his support to candidates like Holconius.

Thinking point 5: There is no evidence that Caecilius ever stood as a candidate, and we have imagined that he much preferred concentrating on his businesses. Create a pros and cons list of standing for election in Pompeii. Do you think you would have wanted to do it if you were eligible?

We know that the Temple of Fortuna Augusta, situated just to the north of the forum, was built largely by the generosity of Marcus Tullius, who owned the whole of the site on which it was built.

Pompeii was free to run its own affairs, but if the local officials were unable to preserve law and order, the central government at Rome might take over and run the town. This actually happened after the famous riot at a gladiatorial show given by Livineius Regulus in AD 59 (described in Stage 8). The Nucerians complained to the Emperor Nero, who banned games in Pompeii for ten years and sent Regulus himself into exile.

Thinking point 6: What does the aftermath of the riot in AD 59 suggest about the balance of power between Pompeii and Rome?

The town council might erect a statue to a leading politician. This is M. Holconius Rufus.

Election notices

It's not just private individuals like me and Quintus who create political notices; in fact most of the slogans are organised by the agents of the candidates and groups of their supporters. In addition to those created on behalf of a candidate's personal friends and clients, a lot of the notices are put up by or to appeal to certain groups of tradespeople or residents of different districts of the city. I've seen notices calling on all kinds of people including barbers, mule drivers, bakers and fishermen to vote for particular candidates.

Many of the thousands of pieces of graffiti found in Pompeii refer to the elections held in March, AD 79. Sometimes appeals were made to particular trade groups as Lucia mentions, for example:

'Innkeepers, vote for Sallustius Capito!'

This picture is based on the graffiti found on a real section of wall in Pompeii. At the top right there is part of a notice advertising a fight of ten pairs of gladiators. It may have been paid for by a candidate in the elections.

Such methods naturally invited replies by rival supporters. One candidate, Vatia, was made to look ridiculous by notices declaring that the 'people who are fast asleep,' 'late drinkers' and 'petty thieves' all supported him.

Thinking point 7: Do people express support (or dislike!) for candidates in modern elections in a similar manner? By what methods?

Even though women can't vote or stand for public office, plenty of us still take a real interest in local politics and express support for our favourite candidates. Here are two examples of graffiti I've noticed recently:

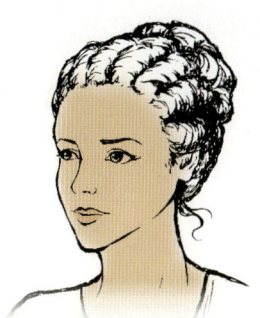

'Parthenope and Rufinus ask for Helvius Sabinus as aedile.'
'Vote for Lucius Popidius Secundus as aedile. It's Taedia Secunda, his grandmother, who asks you to do so'.

Lots of tradeswomen are interested in the elections as well; there are notices from female laundry workers, innkeepers and bakers announcing their political favourites.

It appears that these notices were often painted on the walls at night by lantern light when the streets were quiet, as there was less risk of trouble from rival supporters and it was also easier to put up a ladder without causing congestion on the pavements. Since they were painted these notices should correctly be called 'dipinti'; strictly speaking, ancient 'graffiti' are scratched into the wall.

Thinking point 8: Why do you think women expressed their opinions in political slogans even though they could not vote?

Enquiry: How democratic were local politics in Pompeii?

You may wish to consider the following:

- who could vote and stand for election, and who could not
- the role of the town council
- campaigning
- how much the people of Pompeii engaged with elections
- the relationship with Rome.

Vocabulary checklist 11

cīvis	citizen	**noster**	our
convenit: convēnit	gathers, meets	**nunc**	now
crēdit: crēdidit	trusts, believes	**placet: placuit**	it pleases
dē	about; down from	**prīmus**	first
favet: fāvit	favours, supports	**prōmittit: prōmīsit**	promises
igitur	therefore, and so	**pugna**	fight
invītat: invītāvit	invites	**senātor**	senator
it: iit	goes	**sollicitus**	troubled, anxious
legit: lēgit	reads	**stultus**	foolish
līberālis	generous	**valē!**	goodbye!
minimē!	definitely not! no!	**verberat: verberāvit**	strikes, beats
mūrus	wall	**vir**	man

L. Ceius Secundus is proposed for aedile.

mōns īrātus

1 Clāra et Fēlīx in portū stābant.
amīcī montem spectābant.

2 Clāra amīcō dīxit,
'ego in forō eram.
ego subitō sonōs audīvī.'

3 Fēlīx artificī respondit,
'tū sonōs audīvistī. ego tremōrēs sēnsī.
ego prope montem ambulābam.'

4 Poppaea et Lucriō in ātriō stābant.
sollicitī erant.

5 Poppaea Lucriōnī dīxit,
'ego tibi togam quaerēbam.
ego nūbem mīrābilem cōnspexī.'

6 Lucriō Poppaeae respondit,
'tū nūbem cōnspexistī. sed ego cinerem
sēnsī. ego flammās vīdī.'

7 Thrasymachus et Diodorus in forō erant.
Alexander ad frātrēs contendit.

8 Alexander frātribus dīxit,
'ego ad theātrum contendēbam.
ego sonōs audīvī et tremōrēs sēnsī.
vōs sonōs audīvistis? vōs tremōrēs
sēnsistis?'

9 frātrēs Alexandrō respondērunt,
'nōs tremōrēs sēnsimus et sonōs
audīvimus. nōs nūbem mīrābilem vīdimus.
nōs sollicitī sumus.'

tremōrēs

tremōrēs *earth tremors*

When you have read this story, answer the questions opposite.

Caecilius cum amīcō cēnābat. amīcus in vīllā splendidā prope Nūceriam manēbat. amicus erat Barbillus, mercātor dīves.

> Barbillus Caeciliō dīxit, 'ego sollicitus sum. ego in hortō herī ambulābam et librum legēbam. subitō terra valdē tremuit. ego tremōrēs sēnsī. quid tū agēbās?'

> 'ego servō epistulās dictābam,' inquit Caecilius. 'ego quoque tremōrēs sēnsī. postquam terra tremuit, Grumiō tablīnum intrāvit et mē ad hortum dūxit. nōs nūbem mīrābilem vīdimus.'

> 'vōsne timēbātis?' rogāvit mercātor.

> 'nōs nōn timēbāmus,' Caecilius Barbillō respondit. 'ego, postquam nūbem cōnspexī, familiam meam ad larārium vocāvī. tum nōs laribus sacrificium fēcimus.'

> 'hercle! vōs fortissimī erātis,' clāmāvit mercātor. 'vōs tremōrēs sēnsistis, vōs nūbem cōnspexistis. vōs tamen nōn erātis perterritī.'

> 'nōs nōn timēbāmus, quod nōs laribus crēdēbāmus,' inquit Caecilius. 'iamprīdem terra tremuit. iamprīdem tremōrēs vīllās et mūrōs dēlēvērunt. sed larēs vīllam meam et familiam meam servāvērunt. ego igitur sollicitus nōn sum.'

> subitō servus trīclīnium intrāvit.

> 'domine, Clēmēns est in ātriō. Clēmēns ex urbe vēnit. Caecilium quaerit,' servus Barbillō dīxit.

> 'nōn intellegō,' Caecilius exclāmāvit. 'ego Clēmentem ad fundum meum māne mīsī.'

> servus Clēmentem in trīclīnium dūxit.

> 'cūr tū ē fundō discessistī? cūr tū ad hanc vīllam vēnistī?' rogāvit Caecilius.

> Clēmēns dominō et Barbillō rem tōtam nārrāvit.

dīves *rich*

tremuit *shook*
sēnsī *felt*
agēbās *were doing*
dictābam *was dictating*
nūbem *cloud*
vōsne timēbātis?
   were you afraid?
larārium *lararium*
   *(shrine of the household
   gods)*
sacrificium *sacrifice*

iamprīdem *a long time ago*

fundum *farm*

5

10

15

20

25

At the time of the eruption, Caecilius' lararium was decorated with marble pictures of the earthquake that happened in AD 62 or 63.

Questions

1   **Caecilius cum amīcō cēnābat. amīcus in vīllā splendidā prope Nūceriam manēbat** (lines 1–2): what two things are we told about the house Caecilius' friend was staying in?

2   **'ego sollicitus sum. ego in hortō herī ambulābam et librum legēbam. subitō terra valdē tremuit. ego tremōrēs sēnsī** (lines 3–5): which two of the following statements about Barbillus are true?

   A   He was not worried.

   B   He was sitting in his garden the day before.

   C   He was reading a book.

   D   He felt the earth tremors.

3   **'ego servō epistulās dictābam,' inquit Caecilius. 'ego quoque tremōrēs sēnsī'** (lines 6–7): what was Caecilius doing when he felt the earth tremors?

4   **'postquam terra tremuit, Grumiō tablīnum intrāvit et mē ad hortum dūxit. nōs nūbem mīrābilem vīdimus'** (lines 7–8): write down the two Latin words that indicate what Caecilius and Grumio saw from the garden.

5   **'ego, postquam nūbem cōnspexī, familiam meam ad larārium vocāvī. tum nōs laribus sacrificium fēcimus'** (lines 10–12): what two things happened after Caecilius saw the cloud?

6   **'nōs nōn timēbāmus, quod nōs laribus crēdēbāmus,' inquit Caecilius** (lines 16–17): explain why Caecilius and his household were not afraid.

7   **'iamprīdem terra tremuit. iamprīdem tremōrēs vīllās et mūrōs dēlēvērunt. sed larēs vīllam meam et familiam meam servāvērunt'** (lines 17–19): which three of the following statements are true?

   A   There was an earth tremor that morning.

   B   There was an earth tremor a long time ago.

   C   The earth tremors shook the walls of the houses.

   D   The earth tremors destroyed houses and walls.

   E   Caecilius' house and household were saved.

   F   Caecilius' house and household were lost.

8   **'domine, Clēmēns est in ātriō. Clēmēns ex urbe vēnit. Caecilium quaerit,' servus Barbillō dīxit** (lines 21–22): what three things did the slave tell Barbillus about Clemens?

9   Look at lines 23–24 (**'nōn intellegō,' Caecilius exclāmāvit. 'ego Clēmentem ad fundum meum māne mīsī'**). Where did Caecilius expect Clemens to be?

10 **Clēmēns dominō et Barbillō rem tōtam nārrāvit** (line 28): write down the Latin words that indicate who Clemens told his story to.

ad urbem

'ego ad fundum tuum contendī,' Clēmēns dominō dīxit. 'ego vīlicō epistulam tuam trādidī. postquam vīlicus epistulam lēgit, nōs fundum et servōs īnspiciēbāmus. subitō nōs ingentēs sonōs audīvimus. nōs tremōrēs quoque sēnsimus. tum ego montem spectāvī et nūbem mīrābilem vīdī.'

'quid vōs fēcistis?' rogāvit Barbillus.

'nōs urbem petīvimus, quod valdē timēbāmus,' respondit Clēmēns. 'ego, postquam urbem intrāvī, ingentem clāmōrem audīvī. multī Pompēiānī per viās currēbant. fēminae cum īnfantibus per urbem festīnābant. fīliī et fīliae parentēs quaerēbant. ego ad vīllam nostram pervēnī, ubi Metella manēbat. Metella mē ad tē mīsit, quod nōs perterritī erāmus.'

Caecilius ad urbem contendit, quod sollicitus erat. mercātor et Clēmēns quoque ad urbem festīnāvērunt. maxima turba viās complēbat, quod Pompēiānī ē vīllīs festīnābant.

prope urbem Holcōnium cōnspexērunt. Holcōnius cum servīs ad portum fugiēbat.

'cūr vōs ad urbem contenditis? cūr nōn ad portum fugitis?' rogāvit Holcōnius.

'ad vīllam meam contendō,' Caecilius Holcōniō respondit. 'Metellam et līberōs quaerō. tūne Metellam vīdistī? Quīntum et Lūciam cōnspexistī?'

'ēheu!' clāmāvit Holcōnius. 'ego vīllam splendidam habēbam. in vīllā erant statuae pulchrae et pictūrae pretiōsae. iste mōns vīllam meam dēlēvit; omnēs statuae sunt frāctae.'

'sed, amīce, tū uxōrem meam vīdistī?' rogāvit Caecilius.

'ego nihil dē Metella sciō. nihil cūrō,' respondit Holcōnius.

'furcifer!' clāmāvit Caecilius. 'tū vīllam tuam āmīsistī. ego familiam meam āmīsī!'

Caecilius, postquam Holcōnium vituperāvit, ad urbem contendit.

vīlicō *farm manager*

sonōs *sounds*

parentēs *parents*
pervēnī *reached, arrived*

5

10

15

20

prētiōsae *precious*
iste mōns
    that (terrible) mountain
sciō *know*
nihil cūrō *I don't care*

25

30

This statuette of a Lar might have been how Caecilius pictured the gods who guarded his household.

ad vīllam

in urbe maximus pavor erat. cinis iam dēnsior incidēbat.
flammae ubīque erant. Caecilius et cēterī, postquam urbem
intrāvērunt, vīllam petēbant. sed iter erat difficile, quod
multī Pompēiānī viās complēbant. Caecilius tamen per viās
fortiter contendēbat.

nūbēs iam dēnsissima erat. subitō Barbillus exclāmāvit,
'vōs ad vīllam festīnāte! ego nōn valeō.'

statim ad terram cecidit exanimātus. Clēmēns
mercātōrem ad templum proximum portāvit.

'tū optimē fēcistī,' Caecilius servō dīxit. 'tū amīcum
meum servāvistī. ego tibi lībertātem prōmittō.'

tum Caecilius ē templō discessit et ad vīllam cucurrit.
Clēmēns cum Barbillō in templō manēbat. tandem
mercātor respīrāvit.

'ubi sumus?' rogāvit.

'sumus tūtī,' Clēmēns Barbillō respondit. 'dea Īsis nōs
servāvit. postquam tū in terram cecidistī, ego tē ad hoc
templum portāvī.'

'tibi maximās grātiās agō, quod tū mē servāvistī,' inquit
mercātor. 'sed ubi est Caecilius?'

'dominus meus ad vīllam contendit,' respondit Clēmēns.

'ēheu! stultissimus est Caecilius!' clāmāvit Barbillus.
'sine dubiō Metella et līberī mortuī sunt. ego ex urbe quam
celerrimē discēdō. tū ad dominum tuum festīnā!'

pavor *panic*	
cinis *ash*	
iam *now*	
dēnsior *thicker*	
5	**incidēbat** *was falling*
	flammae *flames*
	cēterī *the others*
	iter *journey, progress*
	difficile *difficult*
10	**dēnsissima** *very thick*
	nōn valeō *don't feel well*
	cecidit *fell*
	exanimātus *unconscious*
	templum proximum
15	*nearest temple*
	optimē *very well*
	lībertātem *freedom*
	respīrāvit *recovered*
	consciousness
20	**tūtī** *safe*
	dea Īsis *goddess Isis*
	(Egyptian deity)
	sine dubiō *without doubt*

The Temple of Isis, Pompeii.

The goddess Isis, on a ring.

fīnis

iam nūbēs ātra ad terram dēscendēbat; iam cinis dēnsissimus incidēbat. plūrimī Pompēiānī iam dē urbe suā dēspērābant.

Clēmēns tamen nōn dēspērābat, sed vīllam petīvit, quod Caecilium quaerēbat. tandem ad vīllam pervēnit. sollicitus ruīnās spectāvit. tōta vīlla ardēbat. Clēmēns fūmum ubīque vīdit. per ruīnās tamen contendit et Caecilium vocāvit. Caecilius tamen nōn respondit. subitō canis lātrāvit.

servus tablīnum intrāvit, ubi canis erat. Cerberus dominum custōdiēbat. Caecilius erat moribundus. Metella prope eum immōta iacēbat. mūrus sēmirutus eōs paene cēlābat. Clēmēns dominō vīnum dedit. Caecilius, postquam vīnum bibit, sēnsim respīrāvit.

'quid accidit, domine?' rogāvit Clēmēns.

'ego ad vīllam vēnī,' inquit Caecilius. 'vīlla erat dēserta. tum ego ad tablīnum contendēbam. uxōrem meam in tablīnō invēnī. sōla Metella mē exspectābat. subitō terra tremuit et pariēs in nōs incidit. tū es servus bonus et fidēlis. abī! ego tē iubeō. dē vītā meā dēspērō. Metella periit. nunc ego quoque sum moritūrus.'

Clēmēns recūsāvit. in tablīnō manēbat. Caecilius iterum clāmāvit,

'Clēmēns, abī! tē iubeō. fortasse Quīntus et Lūcia superfuērunt. quaere Quīntum! hunc ānulum Quīntō dā!'

Caecilius, postquam Clēmentī ānulum suum trādidit, statim exspīrāvit. Clēmēns dominō 'valē' dīxit et ē vīllā discessit.

Cerberus tamen in vīllā mānsit. dominum frūstrā custōdiēbat.

fīnis *end*

ātra *black*
dēscendēbat
    was coming down
plūrimī *most*

ruīnās *ruins, wreckage*
fūmum *smoke*

5

moribundus *almost dead*
sēmirutus *half-collapsed*

10

sēnsim *gradually*
accidit *happened*

15

pariēs *(inside) wall*
in nōs *onto us*
iubeō *order*
periit *has died, has perished*
moritūrus *going to die*
recūsāvit *refused*
superfuērunt *have survived*
quaere! *look for!*
exspīrāvit *died*

20

25

mānsit *stayed, remained*

About the language

1 In Stage 6 you met the imperfect and perfect tenses:

IMPERFECT		PERFECT	
portābat	*s/he* was carrying*	portāvit	*s/he carried*
portābant	*they were carrying*	portāvērunt	*they carried*

imperfect tense and **perfect tense**: page 88

* 'it' and 'they' (singular) are also possible for any 's/he' form of the verb.

2 In this Stage you have met the imperfect and perfect tenses with 'I', 'you', and 'we':

IMPERFECT			PERFECT		
(ego)	portābam	*I was carrying*	(ego)	portāvī	*I carried*
(tū)	portābas	*you (singular) were carrying*	(tū)	portāvistī	*you (singular) carried*
(nōs)	portābāmus	*we were carrying*	(nōs)	portāvimus	*we carried*
(vōs)	portābātis	*you (plural) were carrying*	(vōs)	portāvistis	*you (plural) carried*

ego, **tū**, **nōs** and **vōs** are used only for emphasis and are usually left out.

3 The full imperfect and perfect tenses are:

IMPERFECT		PERFECT	
(ego)	portābam	(ego)	portāvī
(tū)	portābas	(tū)	portāvistī
	portābat		portāvit
(nōs)	portābāmus	(nōs)	portāvimus
(vōs)	portābātis	(vōs)	portāvistis
	portābant		portāvērunt

4 The words for 'was' and 'were' are as follows:

(ego)	eram	*I was*	(nōs)	erāmus	*we were*
(tū)	erās	*you (singular) were*	(vōs)	erātis	*you (plural) were*
	erat	*s/he was*		erant	*they were*

5 Further examples:

a portāvistis; portābātis; portābāmus

b trāxī; trāxērunt; trāxistī

c docēbant; docuī; docuimus

d erātis; audīvī; trahēbam

For more language practice, turn to About the language: page 214

A Pompeian painting of Vesuvius with its fertile slopes covered with vineyards, as it was when Caecilius knew it.

The mountain erupting in the eighteenth century (left); the crater today (top right); and the view from the sea, with the central cone replaced by two lower summits (bottom right).

The destruction of Pompeii

One night in AD 79 it rained hard, a strong wind blew and earth tremors were felt. During the following morning, Vesuvius, which had been an inactive volcano for many centuries, erupted with enormous violence, devastating much of the surrounding area.

The area covered by ash from the eruption.

The traditional date given for the eruption of AD 79 is the 24th August, but more recent archaeological evidence has suggested it was in fact later in the autumn, probably October. One of our most important sources for the eruption is an account written by Pliny the Younger, but we only have medieval copies of this and the date given in each of them varies. Archaeological evidence can help us to work out a likely date, though. We found carbonised remains of ripe pomegranates, which are harvested in autumn, and there was also a lot of wine in storage jars in the vineyards, suggesting that the grape harvest was carried out just before the eruption.

Thinking point 1: Why do some people now question the traditional date of the eruption?

Seventeen-year-old Pliny (the Younger) was staying with his uncle (Pliny the Elder) and later wrote two letters to the historian Tacitus, giving an account of the eruption and its aftermath, including his uncle's tragic death.

'A cloud was rising up – it wasn't clear to those viewing it from a distance which mountain it was coming from, although it was later found to have been Vesuvius. Its shape was more like a pine than any other tree. For it rose up high with, as it were, a very long trunk and then spread out with several branches.'

Pliny refers to the cloud looking like an Italian stone or umbrella pine such as the one above (with Vesuvius looming in the background). Volcanoes which emit clouds like this (for example, the second image) are still called Plinian by scientists.

A huge pyroclastic flow – a massive, superheated and fast-moving cloud of gas, ash and volcanic debris – poured down the mountainside, swallowed the town of Herculaneum, then hardened, sealing the town in solid volcanic rock. In Pompeii, hot stones and ash descended in vast quantities, burying everything to a depth of 4½ to 6 metres (15–20 feet). Pompeii was then also hit by pyroclastic flows.

People working to clear away the huge amounts of volcanic material burying Pompeii. To get a sense of how deep the material is, look at the right hand side of the picture; can you spot the very top of an arch?
This was once a doorway and is now totally blocked up.

'... the courtyard from which his room was reached was now so full of a mixture of ash and pumice and its floor level had risen so much that, if he had delayed any longer in the bedroom, any way out would have been impossible.'

Thinking point 2: Summarise the key difference between the destruction created by Vesuvius in Pompeii and Herculaneum. How might this have affected the later work of archaeologists trying to uncover evidence?

Most people, with vivid memories of the earthquake years before in AD 62, fled into the open countryside carrying a few possessions, but some remained behind, hoping that the storm would pass. They died, buried in the ruins of their homes or killed by the suffocating gas and intense heat of a pyroclastic flow.

'Lying on a linen sheet put down for him, he asked time and again for cold water which he drained down. ... Leaning on two enslaved boys, he got up but at once fell down again, because I imagine, the fumes were thicker, his breathing was obstructed and his windpipe closed up ... When daylight returned (the third day after his last) his body was found intact, uninjured and covered just as he had been dressed; the body looked more like that of someone asleep than dead.'

The next day, here and there the tops of buildings could be seen, and little groups of survivors struggled back to salvage what they could. They dug tunnels to get down to their homes and rescue money, furniture and other valuables, but nothing could be done to excavate and rebuild the town itself.

'At last the darkness thinned as though it disappeared into smoke and cloud; soon real daylight returned, even the sun shone, however it was yellowish as it is in an eclipse. Everything which our frightened eyes encountered was changed and buried deep in ash like in snow.'

Thinking point 3: Using the extracts from Pliny, make a list of the features of the eruption of Vesuvius and how these created such destruction in Pompeii.

The site was abandoned; thousands of refugees made new homes in Naples and other Campanian towns. Gradually the ruins collapsed, a new layer of soil covered the site, and Pompeii disappeared from view. During the Middle Ages, nobody knew exactly where the town lay. Only a vague memory survived in the name 'città' by which the local people still called the low hill.

A table is still in place in an upper room.

Herculaneum: in the foreground are some of the excavated Roman buildings. The modern buildings in the distance lie above the unexcavated part of the town. The second floor of houses survives here.

> **Thinking point 4:** Why do you think Pompeii was lost? Are you surprised people stopped telling the story and forgot where it was?

The rediscovery of Pompeii and Herculaneum

The first remains of Pompeii were found in 1594 when a water channel from the river Sarno to a nearby town was being constructed, but they were not identified as being part of the lost town. An inscription bearing the name of Pompeii was found in 1689, but this was misunderstood as evidence of a villa belonging to the famous Roman politician, Pompeius. Nothing much was done for another 150 years until in 1748 Charles III, king of Naples, began to excavate the site in search of treasure. In 1763, the treasure seekers found another inscription, which read

'REI PUBLICAE POMPEIANORUM'

– *city of the Pompeians* – and they realised they were exploring the lost city of Pompeii.

In the early days, no effort was made to uncover the sites in an orderly way. The people in charge were military engineers, not archaeologists. They were not interested in learning about life in Pompeii; they were looking for jewellery, statues and other works of art to decorate the palaces of kings and rich men. For example, in 1709 a farmer digging a well uncovered several large marble fragments from the Roman theatre of Herculaneum. These fragments were bought to decorate a palace for Prince d'Elbeuf in Portici, Naples. Charles III then continued the excavations to decorate *his* palace at Portici.

At the beginning of the nineteenth century the looting stopped and systematic excavation began. The most fragile and precious objects were taken to the National Museum in Naples, but everything else was kept where it was found. As buildings were uncovered, they were partly reconstructed to preserve them and make them safe for visitors.

Thinking point 5: What impact do you think the actions of the people in the eighteenth century had on the work of more modern archaeologists?

Excavations at Herculaneum were slow and dangerous; the material in the pyroclastic flow had turned to hard rock and the town lay up to 12 metres (40 feet) below the new ground level. This rock created an airtight seal over the town, though, meaning perishable objects have survived intact: for example, wooden doors and stairs, cloth and fishermen's nets. This was not the case at Pompeii, where such material rotted away. This process did, however, leave hollow spaces in the solidified ash. To find out what these had been archaeologists poured liquid plaster into them and then, once it had hardened, carefully removed the surrounding ash to reveal an image of the original object. Casts have been made of many wooden doors and shutters, as well as bodies of human beings and animals.

Thinking point 6: Why did perishable objects survive in Herculaneum but not in Pompeii?

Uncovering the Temple of Isis in 1765.

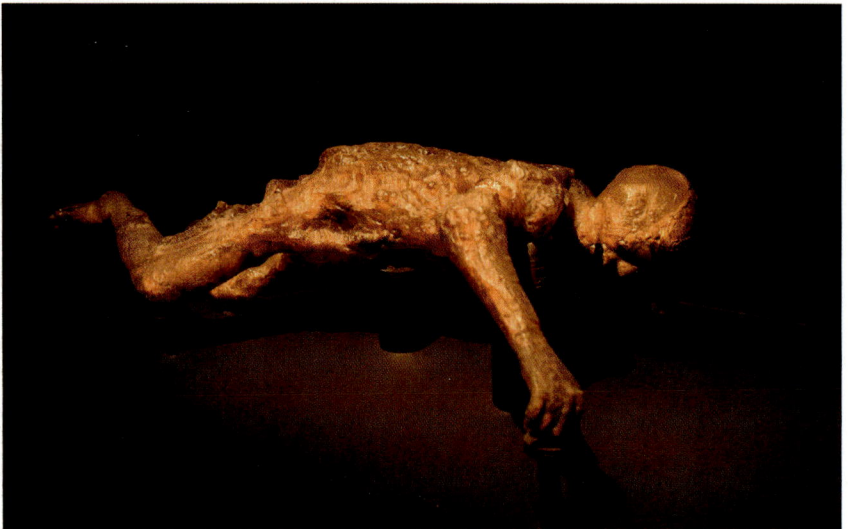

A resin cast of a young woman's body. Unlike plaster, resin is transparent, and bones and jewellery can be seen through it.

Examples of plaster casts from Pompeii.

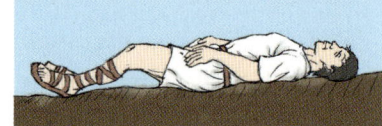
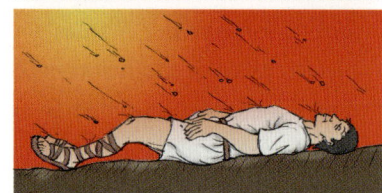

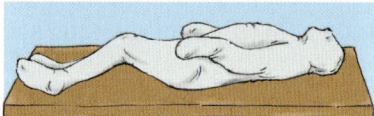

When people died in the eruption their bodies were buried by debris. Over time the bodies decomposed leaving a person-shaped hole in the now solid volcanic material. Archaeologists fill the holes with plaster or resin and then remove the surrounding material to reveal casts such as those in the photographs on this page.

Recently the casts have been laser-scanned by Dr Estelle Lazer, and her work has suggested that many of the original assumptions about them might have been incorrect. For example, an 'old beggar' turned out to be more probably a rich, young man. The scans also showed that the casts were altered to make them more 'relatable' for the public, for example, adding details of facial features, folds in clothing and even missing limbs.

Thinking point 7: Why do you think the casts were altered to make them more 'relatable'? Are you surprised people did this?

This skeleton was discovered at Herculaneum in 1982. The bones showed that she was a woman of about 45, with a protruding jaw; she had gum disease, but no cavities in her teeth. Her wealth was clear from her rings, and the bracelets and earrings that had been in her purse. By contrast, the bones of people who were probably enslaved show signs of overwork and undernourishment.

Through the efforts of archaeologists, a remarkably detailed picture of the life of this ordinary Roman town has emerged from the disaster which destroyed it 2000 years ago. The work is not finished, however; only about two-thirds of Pompeii has so far been uncovered and far less of Herculaneum.

Whenever a new house is opened up, the archaeologists find it just as it was abandoned. We may discover the remains of a meal, pots on the stove, coins in the tablinum, wall paintings (often only slightly damaged), the lead pipes which supplied water to the fountains in the garden, brooches, needles, jars of cosmetics and toys; in fact, all the hundreds of small things that made up a Roman home. If we are lucky, we may also discover the name of the family that lived there, for example, that of Lucius Caecilius Iucundus.

Enquiry: How useful are the sites of Pompeii and Herculaneum for historians studying everyday life in Roman towns?

You may wish to consider the following:

- the nature of the eruption and the types of evidence it preserved
- the types of people we can study using this evidence and why this is unusual
- the history of the site and how it was excavated
- the creation of casts
- the limitations of the evidence.

Vocabulary checklist 12

āmittit: āmīsit	*loses*	**mōns**	*mountain*
bonus	*good, worthy*	**optimē**	*very well*
complet: complēvit	*fills*	**paene**	*nearly, almost*
custōdit: custōdīvit	*guards*	**sentit: sēnsit**	*feels*
epistula	*letter*	**tandem**	*at last*
flamma	*flame*	**templum**	*temple*
fortiter	*bravely*	**terra**	*ground, land*
frūstrā	*in vain*	**timet: timuit**	*is afraid, fears*
fugit: fūgit	*runs away, flees*		
fundus	*farm*		
iacet: iacuit	*lies*		
iam	*now*		
mīrābilis	*strange, extraordinary*		
mittit: mīsit	*sends*		

You have also met these numbers:

ūnus	*one*
duo	*two*
trēs	*three*

An abandoned lantern, with the bones of its owner.

Contents

Part One: About the language

Nouns

1 Words like **puella**, **amīcus**, **mercātor** and **leō** are known as **nouns**.
Nouns are used to indicate people, places or things.

2 In Latin, the ending of the noun indicates the role it is playing in a sentence.
These different forms of the same noun are called **cases**.

3 Each Latin noun belongs to a group called a **declension**.
Each declension has its own set of endings for each case.

4 In Book I, you have met four cases and three declensions:

	first declension	*second declension*	*third declension*	
SINGULAR				
nominative	puella	amīcus	mercātor	leō
accusative	puellam	amīcum	mercātōrem	leōnem
dative	puellae	amīcō	mercātōrī	leōnī
*ablative**	puellā	amīcō	mercātōre	leōne
PLURAL				
nominative	puellae	amīcī	mercātōrēs	leōnēs
accusative	puellās	amīcōs	mercātōres	leōnēs
dative	puellīs	amīcīs	mercātōribus	leōnibus
*ablative**	puellīs	amīcīs	mercātōribus	leōnibus

* In Book I, you have seen the **ablative case** used in phrases such as **in vīllā** and **cum līberīs**,
where a preposition is used with a noun in the ablative case. For more details, see page 185.

5 Review the way the cases are used:

The **nominative case** is used for a noun which is doing the action of the verb.
This noun is known as the subject of the sentence:

mercātor labōrābat.	***The merchant*** *was working.*
amīcī cantābant.	***The friends*** *were singing.*

The nominative case is also used for nouns when they are used with the verb **est**:

Metella est **māter**.	*Metella is **the mother**.*
Āfer et Holcōnius sunt **candidātī**.	*Afer and Holconius are **candidates**.*

The **accusative case** is used for a noun which has the action of the main verb done to it. This noun is known as the direct object of the sentence:

Caecilius **tōnsōrem** salūtāvit.   *Caecilius greeted **the barber**.*
Lūcia **amīcōs** spectābat.   *Lucia was watching **the friends**.*

The **dative case** is used for a noun that is often preceded by the words **to** or **for** in English. This noun is known as the indirect object of the sentence:

Clāra **mercātōrī** pictūram ostendit.
*Clara showed the painting **to the merchant**.*
Or
*Clara showed **the merchant** the painting*

lībertī **amīcīs** vīnum ferēbant.
*The freedmen were bringing the wine **for the friends**.*
Or
*The freedmen were bringing **the friends** the wine.*

Some Latin verbs are always used with a noun in the dative case (rather than the accusative case), even when **to** or **for** are not needed when translating into English:

cīvēs **mercātōrī** crēdunt.   *The citizens trust **the merchant**.*
pistōrēs **Āfrō** favent.   *The bakers support **Afer**.*

6   In each sentence below, change the word in **bold** type from the singular to the plural, and then translate the new sentence.

For example: puerī **amīcum** vīdērunt.
This becomes: puerī **amīcōs** vīdērunt.
Translation: *The boys saw the friends.*

a   puerī **leōnem** vīdērunt.   d   cīvis **amīcō** pecūniam trādidit.

b   pater **puellam** audīvit.   e   coquus **mercātōrī** cēnam parāvit.

c   centuriō **fīlium** salūtāvit.   f   agricolae **gladiātōrem** laudāvērunt.

7   In each sentence below, change the word in **bold** type from the plural to the singular, and then translate the new sentence.

For example: argentāriī **mercātōribus** pecūniam dedērunt.
This becomes: argentāriī **mercātōrī** pecūniam dedērunt.
Translation: *The bankers gave money to the merchant.*

a   spectātor **amīcōs** salūtāvit.   d   gladiātōrēs **leōnibus** cibum dedērunt.

b   āthlētae **mercātōrēs** vituperāvērunt.   e   iuvenēs **amīcīs** statuam trādidērunt.

c   Lūcia **puellās** audiēbat.   f   cīvēs **āctōribus** fāvērunt.

Verbs

1 Words like **portō**, **doceō**, **trahō** and **audiō** are known as **verbs**.
Verbs are used to express an action.

2 In Latin, the ending of the verb indicates who is doing the action.

3 Different forms of the same verb are used to indicate when the action occurs.
These different forms are known as **tenses**.

4 In Book I, you have met three tenses:

PRESENT TENSE	portō	*I carry*
	portās	*you (singular) carry*
	portat	*s/he* carries*
	portāmus	*we carry*
	portātis	*you (plural) carry*
	portant	*they carry*
IMPERFECT TENSE	portābam	*I was carrying*
	portābās	*you (singular) were carrying*
	portābat	*s/he was carrying*
	portābāmus	*we were carrying*
	portābātis	*you (plural) were carrying*
	portābant	*they were carrying*
PERFECT TENSE	portāvī	*I carried*
	portāvistī	*you (singular) carried*
	portāvit	*s/he carried*
	portāvimus	*we carried*
	portāvistis	*you (plural) carried*
	portāvērunt	*they carried*

* 'it' and 'they' (singular) are also possible for any 's/he' form of the verb.

5 English has more than one way of translating each of these tenses.

- **portō** can mean *I carry* or *I am carrying*. The present tense indicates an action happening at the present time.

- **portābam** can mean *I was carrying, I used to carry* or *I began to carry*. The imperfect tense indicates an ongoing, repeated or incomplete action in past time.

- **portāvī** can mean *I carried* or *I have carried*. The perfect tense indicates a single or complete action in past time.

6 Just as nouns belong to declensions, verbs belong to groups known as **conjugations**.

- **portō** *I carry* is an example of a first conjugation verb.
  Further examples: **ambulō** and **labōrō**.

- **doceō** *I teach* is an example of a second conjugation verb.
  Further examples: **sedeō** and **videō**.

- **trahō** *I drag* is an example of a third conjugation verb.
  Further examples: **currō** and **dīcō**.

- **audiō** *I hear* is an example of a fourth conjugation verb.
  Further examples: **dormiō** and **veniō**.

7 The full table of verb endings met in Book I is as follows:

	first conjugation	*second conjugation*	*third conjugation*	*fourth conjugation*
PRESENT TENSE	portō	doceō	trahō	audiō
	portās	docēs	trahis	audīs
	portat	docet	trahit	audit
	portāmus	docēmus	trahimus	audīmus
	portātis	docētis	trahitis	audītis
	portant	docent	trahunt	audiunt
IMPERFECT TENSE	portābam	docēbam	trahēbam	audiēbam
	portābās	docēbās	trahēbās	audiēbās
	portābat	docēbat	trahēbat	audiēbat
	portābāmus	docēbāmus	trahēbāmus	audiēbāmus
	portābātis	docēbātis	trahēbātis	audiēbātis
	portābant	docēbant	trahēbant	audiēbant
PERFECT TENSE	portāvī	docuī	trāxī	audīvī
	portāvistī	docuistī	trāxistī	audīvistī
	portāvit	docuit	trāxit	audīvit
	portāvimus	docuimus	trāximus	audīvimus
	portāvistis	docuistis	trāxistis	audīvistis
	portāvērunt	docuērunt	trāxērunt	audīvērunt

8 In the table on the previous page, find the Latin words for:

    a I teach; we drag; he hears.

    b She was dragging; you (plural) were teaching; they were carrying.

    c He heard; they dragged; we taught.

    d We heard; you (sing.) teach; they were dragging; she carried.

9 Most verbs in the first, second and fourth conjugations form their perfect tenses in the following ways:

    First conjugation: like **portāvī**, e.g. **salūtāvī**, **spectāvī**
    Second conjugation: like **docuī**, e.g. **terruī**, **appāruī**
    Fourth conjugation: like **audīvī**, e.g. **dormīvī**, **custōdīvī**.

10 Some verbs in the third conjugation form their perfect tense in the same way as **trāxī**, e.g. **dūxī**, **intellēxī**. But there are many other ways in which verbs may form their perfect tense, especially in the third conjugation. Note the following patterns:

    a A consonant change, most often with **s** or **x**:

PRESENT		PERFECT	
discēdit	*s/he leaves*	disce**ss**it	*s/he left*
mittit	*s/he sends*	mī**s**it	*s/he sent*
scrībit	*s/he writes*	scrī**ps**it	*s/he wrote*
dīcit	*s/he says*	dī**x**it	*s/he said*

    b A vowel change:

PRESENT		PERFECT	
facit	*s/he makes*	f**ē**cit	*s/he made*
capit	*s/he takes*	c**ē**pit	*s/he took*

    c Adding an extra syllable:

PRESENT		PERFECT	
currit	*s/he runs*	**cu**currit	*s/he ran*
dat	*s/he gives*	**de**dit	*s/he gave*

d Changing the pronunciation (a change of vowel sound, shown by placing a line above the vowel):

PRESENT		PERFECT	
venit	*s/he comes*	vēnit	*s/he came*
fugit	*s/he flees*	fūgit	*s/he fled*

e No change:

PRESENT		PERFECT	
ostendit	*s/he shows*	ostendit	*s/he showed*
contendit	*s/he hurries*	contendit	*s/he hurried*

11 Translate these examples:

a ego sedeō; puella sedet; nōs sedēmus; amīcī sedent.

b mercātōrēs labōrābant; tū labōrābās; mercātor labōrābat; ego labōrābam.

c canēs dormīvērunt; tū dormīvistī; dormīvit; nōs dormīvimus.

d agricolae cucurrērunt; vōs cucurristis; cucurrī; Melissa cucurrit.

e amīcus clāmat; amīcus clāmābat; amīcus clāmāvit.

f clāmās; clāmābat; clāmāvistis.

g dīcō; dīcēbāmus; dīxistī.

h vidēmus; currēbās; veniēbant; ambulāvī.

12 A few verbs which do not belong to any of the four conjugations are known as **irregular verbs**. This is the most important one:

PRESENT TENSE		IMPERFECT TENSE	
sum	*I am*	eram	*I was*
es	*you (sing.) are*	erās	*you (sing.) were*
est	*s/he is*	erat	*s/he was*
sumus	*we are*	erāmus	*we were*
estis	*you (plural) are*	erātis	*you (plural) were*
sunt	*they are*	erant	*they were*

Word order

1   The following word order is very common in Latin:

      Milō discum īnspexit.   *Milo looked at the discus.*
      mercātor togam vēndidit.   *The merchant sold the toga.*

2   From Stage 7 onwards, you have met a slightly different example:

      discum īnspexit.   *He looked at the discus.*
      togam vēndidit.   *He sold the toga.*
      amīcum salūtāvit.   *She greeted her friend.*
      theātrum intrāvērunt.   *They entered the theatre.*

3   The following sentences are similar to those in paragraphs 1 and 2:

    a spectātōrēs Milōnem laudāvērunt.   **g** poētam vīdit.

    b Milōnem laudāvērunt.   **h** āthlētam salūtāvit.

    c artifex Lūciam cōnspexit.   **i** mē salūtāvit.

    d Lūciam cōnspexit.   **j** tē salūtāvērunt.

    e canēs et cīvēs leōnem necāvērunt.   **k** Metella clāmōrem audīvit.

    f mercātor poētam et tōnsōrem vīdit.   **l** clāmōrem audīvit.

4   Further examples:

    a Caecilius amīcum salūtat; amīcum salūtat.

    b ego amīcōs salūtāvī; amīcōs salūtāvī.

    c nōs gladiātōrēs spectābāmus; clāmōrem audīvimus.

    d vōs pāvōnem cōnsūmēbātis; vīnum bibēbātis; cibum laudāvistis.

5   From Stage 9 onwards, you have met longer sentences, involving the dative.
    The following word order is common in Latin:

      Metella Lūciae dōnum trādidit.
      Metella handed over a gift to Lucia.

6   Further examples:

    a iuvenis Milōnī discum trādidit.   **d** nūntiī cīvibus spectāculum nūntiāvērunt.

    b Metella fīliō togam ēmit.   **e** Quīntus mercātōrī et amīcīs togam ostendit.

    c Rēgulus gladiātōribus signum dedit.   **f** Caecilius Lūciae librum quaerēbat.

Longer sentences with *postquam* and *quod*

1 Compare these two sentences:

Pompēiānī gladiātōrēs vīdērunt.
The Pompeians saw the gladiators.

Pompēiānī, postquam amphitheātrum intrāvērunt, gladiātōrēs vīdērunt.
The Pompeians, after they entered the amphitheatre, saw the gladiators.
Or, in more natural English:
After the Pompeians entered the amphitheatre, they saw the gladiators.

2 The next example is similar:

amīcī umbram timēbant.
The friends were afraid of the ghost.

amīcī, quod erant ignāvī, umbram timēbant.
The friends, because they were cowardly, were afraid of the ghost.
Or:
Because the friends were cowardly, they were afraid of the ghost.

3 Further examples:

a Metella ad tablīnum festīnāvit.
Metella, postquam ē culīnā discessit, ad tablīnum festīnāvit.

b amīcī Fēlīcem laudāvērunt.
amīcī, postquam fābulam audīvērunt, Fēlīcem laudāvērunt.

c tuba sonuit.
postquam Rēgulus signum dedit, tuba sonuit.

d Caecilius nōn erat sollicitus.
Caecilius nōn erat sollicitus, quod in cubiculō dormiēbat.

e Nūcerīnī fūgērunt.
Nūcerīnī, quod Pompēiānī erant īrātī, fūgērunt.

Part Two: Reviewing the language

Stage 1

Latin sentences 1

Complete and translate: Complete each Latin sentence with a word or phrase from the box. Then translate your sentence. Use each word or phrase only once.

Latin sentences: page 7

For example: . . . . est in hortō.

              mater est in hortō.

              Mother is in the garden.

1

> Quīntus   Grumiō   Caecilius   canis
> māter   Lūcia   Clēmēns

a . . . . est in cubiculō.

b . . . . est in hortō.

c . . . . est in viā.

d . . . . est in culīnā.

e . . . . est in tablīnō.

f . . . . est in ātriō.

g . . . . est in trīclīniō.

2

> in viā   in hortō   in ātriō   in tablīnō
> in culīnā   in trīclīniō   in cubiculō

a Grumiō . . . . stat.

b Caecilius . . . . scrībit.

c canis . . . . lātrat.

d Metella . . . . legit.

e Lūcia est . . . .

f Quīntus est . . . .

g Clēmēns est . . . .

Stage 2

Latin sentences 2

Complete and translate: Complete each Latin sentence with a word or phrase from the box. Use each word or phrase only once. Then translate your sentence.

Make sure that the sentence you create makes sense.

For example: canis . . . . stat.
                canis **in viā** stat.
                The dog is standing in the street.

scrībit   in culīnā   fīlius   amīcus   legit   in viā

a Grumiō . . . . cantat.

b . . . . in hortō sedet.

c mercātor in tablīnō . . . .

d Cerberus . . . . dormit.

e Metella in ātriō . . . .

f . . . . in trīclīniō cēnat.

Nominatives and accusatives 1

Complete and translate: Complete each Latin sentence with the correct word from the brackets. Then translate the sentence.

Make sure that the sentence you create makes sense.

nominative case and **accusative case**: page 25

For example: amīcus Caecilium . . . . (sedet, vīsitat)
                amīcus Caecilium **vīsitat**.
                A friend visits Caecilius.

a Caecilius pecūniam . . . . (numerat, dormit)

b mercātor vīnum . . . . (labōrat, portat)

c Melissa hortum . . . . (intrat, gustat)

d Metella mercātōrem . . . . (salūtat, cantat)

e Quīntus cibum . . . . (vīsitat, cōnsūmit)

f Cerberus vīllam . . . . (dormit, intrat, portat)

g amīcus Grumiōnem . . . . (spectat, stat, recumbit)

h māter fīlium . . . . (bibit, dormit, vocat)

i Clēmēns canem . . . . (sedet, cōnsūmit, audit)

j pater Lūciam . . . . (scrībit, laudat, numerat)

Stage 3

Latin sentences 3

Complete and translate: Complete each Latin sentence with the correct word from the brackets. Then translate the sentence.

Make sure that the sentence you create makes sense.

a mercātor ē vīllā . . . . (quaerit, ambulat)

b amīcus ad hortum . . . . (recitat, venit)

c Cerberus ad culīnam . . . . (revenit, habet)

d artifex ē trīclīniō . . . . (laudat, exit)

e Grumiō canem ad viam . . . . (dūcit, intrat)

f Lūcia vīnum ad Caecilium . . . . (clāmat, respondet, portat)

Nominatives and accusatives 2

Complete and translate: Complete each Latin sentence with the correct word from the brackets. Then translate the sentence.

Check to see if you need a **nominative** or an **accusative** to complete your sentence.

nominative case and **accusative case**: page 25

For example: . . . . vīnum bibit. (amīcus, amīcum)
amīcus vīnum bibit.
The friend drinks the wine.

a amīcus . . . . laudat. (cibus, cibum)

b senex . . . . intrat. (taberna, tabernam)

c . . . . cibum gustat. (Barbillus, Barbillum)

d . . . . Metellam salūtat. (mercātor, mercātōrem)

e Caecilius . . . . videt. (tōnsor, tōnsōrem)

f . . . . versum recitat. (poēta, poētam)

g . . . . in forō ambulat. (senex, senem)

h Lūcia . . . . ad ātrium dūcit. (artifex, artificem)

Stage 4

Verbs 1

Complete and translate: Complete the second Latin sentence with the correct verb from the brackets. Then translate both sentences.

Make sure that the sentence you create makes sense.

verbs: page 56

a ego sum Metella.

   ego in ātriō . . . . (sedeō, coquō)

b ego sum mercātor.

   ego nāvem . . . . (stō, habeō)

c ego sum Herculēs.

   ego fūstem . . . . (teneō, sedeō)

d ego sum Caecilius.

   ego in hortō . . . . (habeō, ambulō)

e tū es amīcus.

   tū vīllam . . . . (intrās, dūcis)

f tū es mendāx.

   tū pecūniam . . . . (dēbēs, ambulās)

h tū es iūdex.

   tū Hermogenem . . . . (curris, convincis)

i ego sum Clāra.

   ego picturam . . . . (pingō, ambulō)

j tū es senex.

   tū in tabernā . . . . (tenēs, sedēs)

Stage 5

Singulars and plurals 1

Complete and translate: Complete each Latin sentence with the correct verb from the brackets. Then translate the sentence.

For example: senēs . . . . (dormit, dormiunt)
senēs **dormiunt**.
The old men are sleeping.

a āctōrēs . . . . (adest, adsunt)

b puellae in theātrō . . . . (sedent, sedet)

c agricolae ad urbem . . . . (currunt, currit)

d Pompēiānī clāmōrem . . . . (facit, faciunt)

e amīcī ad theātrum . . . . (contendit, contendunt)

Singulars and plurals 2

Complete and translate: Complete each Latin sentence with the correct verb from the brackets. Then translate the sentence.

a pāstōrēs ad theātrum . . . . (contendit, contendunt)

b pāstor pecūniam nōn . . . . (habet, habent)

c puella āctōrem . . . . (laudat, laudant)

d fēminae fābulam . . . . (spectat, spectant)

e puerī ad urbem . . . . (venit, veniunt)

f nūntius in forō . . . . (clāmat, clāmant)

g senēs in forō . . . . (dormit, dormiunt)

h pater . . . . in tablīnō. (est, sunt)

Check the **nominative noun** to see if you need a **singular** or a **plural** form of the verb.

singular and plural verbs: page 73

singular and plural nouns: page 75

Check the **nominative noun** to see if you need a **singular** or a **plural** form of the verb.

Stage 6

Verb tenses 1

Complete and translate: Complete each Latin sentence with the correct noun from the brackets. Then translate the sentence. Take care with the meaning of the tenses of the verb.

For example: .... in forō ambulābat. (fīlius, fīliī)
fīlius in forō ambulābat.
The son was walking in the forum.

.... forum intrāvērunt. (amīcus, amīcī)
amīcī forum intrāvērunt.
The friends entered the forum.

a .... per viam festīnābat. (puella, puellae)

b .... pecūniam portābant. (amīcus, amīcī)

c .... ātrium circumspectāvit. (fūr, fūrēs)

d .... clāmōrem audīvērunt. (mercātor, mercātōrēs)

e .... fūrem superāvērunt. (puer, puerī)

f .... ad urbem festīnāvit. (nauta, nautae)

Check the **verb** to see if you need a **singular** or a **plural nominative**.

singular and plural nouns: page 75

verb tenses: page 88

Stage 7

Verb tenses 2

Complete and translate: Complete each sentence with the correct phrase from the brackets. Then translate the sentence.

Check the **nominative noun** to see if you need a **singular** or a **plural** form of the **verb**.

singular and plural nouns: page 75

perfect verbs: page 108

For example: amīcī . . . . (vīllam intrāvit, cēnam laudāvērunt)
amīcī **cēnam laudāvērunt**.
The friends praised the dinner.

a mercātor . . . . (ē vīllā discessit, clāmōrem audīvērunt)

b puellae . . . . (ad vīllam ambulāvit, in vīllā dormīvērunt)

c leōnēs . . . . (gladiātōrem terruit, gladiātōrem cōnspexērunt)

d lībertī . . . . (lūnam spectāvit, ad portum festīnāvērunt)

e centuriō . . . . (fābulam audīvit, cibum laudāvērunt)

f fūr . . . . (per urbem ruit, centuriōnem terruērunt)

g Caecilius et Metella . . . . (leōnem cōnspexit, portum petīvērunt)

h amīcī . . . . (pōculum īnspexit, rem intellēxērunt)

Nominatives and accusatives 3

Complete and translate: Complete each sentence with the correct form of the noun from the brackets. Then translate the sentence.

Check to see if you need a **nominative** or an **accusative** to complete your sentence, and if it should be **singular** or **plural**.

nominatives and accusatives: page 123

For example: Caecilius . . . . spectāvit. (āctor, āctōrem)
Caecilius **āctōrem** spectāvit.
Caecilius watched the actor.

. . . . ad silvam ambulāvērunt.
(amīcus, amīcī)
amīcī ad silvam ambulāvērunt.
The friends walked to the wood.

a   Metella . . . . vocāvit. (Caecilius, Caecilium)

b   . . . . fābulam nārrāvit. (lībertus, lībertum)

c   . . . . gladiātōrem cōnspexērunt. (amīcus, amīcī)

d   . . . . ad forum festīnāvērunt. (agricola, agricolae)

e   fīlia . . . . aperuit. (iānua, iānuam)

f   . . . . clāmōrem fēcit. (puella, puellae)

g   fūrēs . . . . necāvērunt. (centuriō, centuriōnem)

h   . . . . cēnam laudāvit. (gladiātor, gladiātōrem)

i   . . . . cibum ad theātrum portāvērunt. (spectātor, spectātōrēs)

j   . . . . ē vīllā discessit. (senex, senēs)

Stage 8

Verbs 2

Complete and translate: Complete each sentence with the correct word from the box. Then translate the sentence.

Remember to check who is doing the action in each sentence.

verbs: page 56

ego	leōnēs	tū	vēndō	amīcōs	spectās

a . . . . multās vīllās habeō.

b ego vīnum . . . .

c tū gladiātōrēs . . . .

d ego . . . . salūtō.

e . . . . fābulās laudās.

f tū . . . . agitās.

Verbs 3

Complete and translate: Complete each sentence with the correct form of the verb from the brackets. Then translate the sentence.

Check the **nominative noun** to see who is doing the action and choose the correct form of the **verb**.

verbs: page 56

a tū es mercātor;
tū vīnum in forō . . . . (vēndō, vēndis, vēndit)

b ego sum gladiātor;
ego in arēnā . . . . (pugnō, pugnās, pugnat)

c Fēlīx est lībertus; Fēlīx cum Caeciliō . . . . (cēnō, cēnās, cēnat)

d ego multōs spectātōrēs in amphitheātrō . . . . (videō, vidēs, videt)

e tū in vīllā magnificā . . . . (habitō, habitās, habitat)

f Rēgulus hodiē diem nātālem . . . . (celebrō, celebrās, celebrat)

g tū saepe ad amphitheātrum . . . . (veniō, venīs, venit)

h ego rem . . . . (intellegō, intellegis, intellegit)

Stage 9

Datives 1

Complete and translate: Complete each sentence with the verb from the brackets that makes good sense. Then translate the sentence, taking care with the different forms of the nouns.

Make sure that the sentence you create makes sense.

For example: mercātōrēs fēminīs tunicās . . . . (audīvērunt, ostendērunt, timuērunt)
mercātōrēs fēminīs tunicās **ostendērunt**.
The merchants showed the tunics to the women.

a āthlēta amīcō dōnum . . . . (timuit, dedit, salūtāvit)

b iuvenis puellae stolam . . . . (ēmit, vēnit, prōcessit)

c fēminae fīliīs tunicās . . . . (intrāvērunt, quaesīvērunt, contendērunt)

d cīvēs āctōrī pecūniam . . . . (laudāvērunt, vocāvērunt, trādidērunt)

e artifex mercātōribus decem dēnāriōs . . . . (trādidit, ēmit, vīdit)

Datives 2

Complete and translate: Complete each sentence with the correct form of the verb from the brackets. Then translate the sentence.

Check the **nominative noun** to see if you need a **singular** or a **plural verb**.

singular and plural nouns: page 75

verb tenses: page 88

For example:
Quīntus amīcīs togam . . . . (ostendit, ostendērunt)
Quīntus amīcīs togam **ostendit**.
Quintus showed the toga to his friends.

a puella gladiātōribus tunicās . . . . (dedit, dedērunt)

b cīvēs Milōnī statuam . . . . (posuit, posuērunt)

c centuriō amīcō vīnum . . . . (trādidit, trādidērunt)

d Grumiō amīcae ānulum . . . . (ēmit, ēmērunt)

e Lūcia et Clāra Metellae pictūram optimam . . . . (ostendit, ostendērunt)

Stage 10

Verbs 4

Complete and translate: Complete each sentence with the most suitable phrase from the box. Then translate the sentence.

Make sure that the sentence you create makes sense.

> fābulam agimus   contrōversiam habēmus
> vīnum vēndimus   versum recitāvimus   pānem parāmus

a   nōs sumus rhētorēs Graecī; nōs in palaestrā . . . .

b   nōs sumus āctōrēs nōtissimī; nōs in theātrō . . . .

c   nōs sumus poetae callidae; nōs fēminīs . . . .

d   nōs sumus pistōrēs; nōs cīvibus . . . .

e   nōs sumus mercātōrēs; nōs Pompēiānīs . . . .

Verbs 5

Complete and translate: Complete each sentence with the most suitable noun from the box. Then translate the sentence.

Make sure that the sentence you create makes sense.

'we' and 'you': page 162

> mercātōrēs   āthlētae   artificēs   argentāriī   gladiātōrēs

a   vōs estis . . . . callidī; vōs pictūrās magnificās pingitis.

b   vōs estis . . . . fortēs; vōs in arēnā pugnātis.

c   nōs sumus . . . . ; nōs in forō negōtium agimus.

d   vōs vīnum in forō vēnditis, quod vōs estis . . . .

e   nōs ad palaestram contendimus, quod nōs sumus . . . .

Stage 11

Verbs 6

Complete and translate: Complete each sentence with the correct form of the verb from the box. Then translate the sentence. Do not use any word more than once.

Check the **nominative noun** to see who is doing the action. Remember to check that your sentence makes sense.

the whole of the present tense: page 162

> contendō   contendis   contendimus   contenditis
> faveō   favēs   favēmus   favētis

a   ego ad forum . . . . ego sum candidātus.

b   tū Āfrō . . . . tū es stultus.

c   ego Holcōniō . . . ., quod Holcōnius est candidātus optimus.

d   nōs Holcōniō nōn . . . ., quod Holcōnius est asinus.

e   Clēmēns, cūr tū ad portum . . . .?

f   vōs Āfrō . . . ., quod vōs estis pistōrēs.

g   nōs ad vīllam . . . ., quod in forō sunt Holcōnius et amīcī.

h   ēheu! cūr ē forō . . . .? vōs dēnāriōs meōs habētis!

Nominatives and accusatives 4

Complete and translate: Complete each sentence with the correct form of the noun from the brackets. Then translate the sentence.

Check to see if you need a **nominative** or an **accusative** to complete your sentence, and if it should be **singular** or **plural**.

nouns: page 123

a   Quīntus Sullae decem dēnāriōs dedit.
Sulla . . . . in mūrō scrīpsit. (titulus, titulum)

b   fūr thermās intrābat.
. . . . eum agnōvit. (mercātor, mercātōrem)

c   multī candidātī sunt in forō.
ego . . . . videō. (Holcōnius, Holcōnium)

d   ego ad portum currō. . . . . mē exspectat. (amīca, amīcae)

e   hodiē ad urbem contendō. in amphitheātrō sunt . . . . (leō, leōnēs)

f   rhētor est īrātus. rhētor . . . . exspectat. (puerī, puerōs)

g   fēminae sunt in tabernā. mercātōrēs fēminīs . . . . ostendunt. (stolae, stolās)

h   postquam Holcōnius et amīcī Grumiōnem cēpērunt, quīnque . . . . rapuērunt.
(dēnāriī, dēnāriōs)

Part Three: Vocabulary

1 Nouns are usually listed in the nominative singular. For example:

    amīcus   *friend*

2 Third declension nouns, however, are listed in both the nominative and the accusative singular. For example:

    leō: leōnem   *lion*

This means that **leō** is the nominative singular and **leōnem** the accusative singular of the Latin word for 'lion'.

3 *Practice examples*

Find the nominative singular of the following words:

    novāculam

    lupum

    sanguinem

    stēllae

    īnfantēs

    mūrō

    cīvibus

4 Verbs are usually listed in the third person singular of the present and perfect tenses. For example:

    parat: parāvit   *prepares*

This indicates that **parat** means *s/he prepares* and **parāvit** means *s/he prepared* or *has prepared*.

5 If only one of these tenses is used in Book I, then only that tense is listed. For example:

    exspīrāvit   *died*

6 Sometimes, if the perfect tense looks somewhat different from the present tense, it will be listed separately, as well as with its present tense. For example:

    dat: dedit   *gives*

    dedit   *gave*

7 *Practice examples*

Find the meaning of the following words, some of which are in the present tense and some in the perfect:

>   laudat
>
>   laudāvit
>
>   respondit
>
>   respondet
>
>   intellēxit
>
>   accēpit
>
>   salūtāvit
>
>   tenet
>
>   dēposuit
>
>   fūgit

8 Phrases (e.g. **grātiās agit**, **rem intellegit**, etc.) are listed under both words of the phrase.

9 Some Latin words have more than one possible translation. Always choose the most suitable translation for the sentence you are working on.

>   cīvēs perterritī portum **petēbant**.
>   *The terrified citizens **were heading for** the harbour.*
>
>   pistōrēs īrātī mercātōrem **petēbant**.
>   *The angry bakers **were attacking** the merchant.*

10 Where a word appears in a Vocabulary checklist in Stages 1–12, it is marked with the relevant Stage number in the following pages. For example:

>   1   **canis: canem**   *dog*

This means that **canis** appears as a Vocabulary checklist word in Stage 1.

a

6	abest	*is out, is absent*
10	abit: abiit	*goes away*
	accidit	*happened*
10	accipit: accēpit	*accepts*
	accūsat	*accuses*
	āctor: āctōrem	*actor*
3	ad	*to, towards, at*
5	adest	*is here, is present*
	adiuvat	*helps*
	administrat	*manages*
5	adsunt	*are here*
	aedificat	*builds*
	aeger: aegrum	*sick, ill*
	Aegyptius	*Egyptian*
4	agit	*does, acts*
	fābulam agit	*acts out a play*
	grātiās agit	*thanks, is grateful*
	negōtium agit	*does business*
8	agitat: agitāvit	*chases, hunts*
9	agnōscit: agnōvit	*recognises*
5	agricola	*farmer*
	alius	*other, another*
	alter: alterum	*the other, the second*
	amat	*loves*
5	ambulat: ambulāvit	*walks*
	amīca	*(female) friend*
2	amīcus	*(male) friend*
	amīcissimus	*very friendly, very good friend*
12	āmittit: āmīsit	*loses*
	amphitheātrum	*amphitheatre*
2	ancilla	*(female) slave, enslaved woman*
	antīquus	*old, ancient*
4	ānulus	*ring*
	anxius	*worried*
	aper: aprum	*boar*
	aperit: aperuit	*opens*
	apodytērium	*changing room*
	appāruit	*appeared*
	architectus	*builder, architect*

	ardet	*burns, is on fire*
	arēna	*arena*
	argentāria	*banker's stall*
	argentārius	*banker*
	argūmentum	*evidence*
	artifex: artificem	*artist, craftsperson*
	asinus	*donkey*
	āter: ātrum	*black*
	āthlēta	*athlete*
	ātrium	*atrium (reception room)*
	attonitus	*astonished*
	auctor: auctōrem	*creator*
	audācissimē	*very boldly*
	audāx	*bold, courageous*
5	audit: audīvit	*hears, listens to*
	aurae	*air*
	auxilium	*help*
	avārus	*miser (stingy person)*

b

	babae!	*hey!*
	barba	*beard*
	barbarus	*foreigner, barbarian*
	basilica	*law court*
	benignus	*kind, generous*
	bēstia	*wild animal*
	bēstiārius	*beast fighter*
3	bibit: bibit	*drinks*
12	bonus	*good, worthy*

c

	caelum	*sky*
	caldārium	*hot room*
10	callidus	*clever*
	callidior	*more clever*
	callidissimus	*very clever*
	candidātus	*candidate*
1	canis: canem	*dog*
	cantat: cantāvit	*sings*
10	capit: cēpit	*catches, captures, takes*
	caudex: caudicem	*idiot*

	caupō: caupōnem	*innkeeper*
	cautē	*cautiously*
	cavē!	*beware!*
	cecidit	*fell*
	cēlat	*hides*
	celebrat	*celebrates*
9	celeriter	*quickly*
	quam celerrimē	*as quickly as possible*
2	cēna	*dinner*
	cēnat: cēnāvit	*eats dinner, dines*
	centuriō: centuriōnem	*centurion*
10	cēpit	*caught, captured, took*
	cēra	*wax tablet*
	cervus	*deer*
	cēterī	*the others, the rest*
2	cibus	*food*
	cinis: cinerem	*ash*
3	circumspectat: circumspectāvit	*looks round*
11	cīvis: cīvem	*citizen*
3	clāmat: clāmāvit	*shouts*
5	clāmor: clāmōrem	*noise, shouting*
	clausus	*closed*
	columba	*dove, darling*
	commīsit	*began*
	commōtus	*moved, shaken*
12	complet: complēvit	*fills*
	compōnit	*arranges*
	comprehendit	*arrested*
	cōnsentit	*agrees*
	cōnsilium	*plan, idea*
7	cōnspicit: cōnspexit	*catches sight of, notices*
8	cōnsūmit: cōnsūmpsit	*eats*
5	contendit: contendit	*hurries*
	contentiō: contentiōnem	*argument*
10	contentus	*satisfied*
	contrōversia	*debate*
11	convenit: convēnit	*gathers, meets*
	convincit	*convicts, finds guilty*
4	coquit	*cooks*
1	coquus	*cook*

	corrigit: corrēxit	*amends, puts right*
	cotīdiē	*every day*
11	crēdit: crēdidit	*believes in, trusts*
	crīnis: crīnem	*hair*
	cubiculum	*bedroom*
	cucurrit	*ran*
	culīna	*kitchen*
7	cum	*with*
9	cupit: cupīvit	*wants, desires*
4	cūr?	*why?*
	cūrat: cūrāvit	*cares for*
	nihil cūrat	*does not care*
5	currit: cucurrit	*runs*
12	custōdit: custōdīvit	*guards*

d

9	dat: dedit	*gives*
	fābulam dat	*puts on a play*
11	dē	*down from; about*
	dea	*goddess*
	dēbet	*owes*
	decem	*ten*
	dēcipit	*deceives, fools*
9	dedit	*gave*
	dēiēcit	*threw down*
	deinde	*then*
	dēlectat: dēlectāvit	*delights, pleases*
	dēlēvit	*destroyed*
	dēliciae	*sweetheart*
	dēnārius	*denarius (small coin)*
	dēnsus	*thick*
	dēnsior	*thicker*
	dēnsissimus	*very thick*
	dēpōnit: dēposuit	*takes off*
	dēscendit	*comes down*
	dēsertus	*deserted*
	dēsiste!	*stop!*
	dēspērat	*despairs*
	dēstrīnxit	*drew out*
	deus	*god*
	dīcit: dīxit	*says*

	dictat	*dictates*
9	diēs: diem	*day*
	diēs nātālis: diem nātālem	*birthday*
	difficilis	*difficult*
	dīligenter	*carefully*
	discēdit: discessit	*departs, leaves*
	discit	*learns*
	discus	*discus*
	dissentit	*disagrees, argues*
	diū	*for a long time*
	dīves: dīvitem	*rich*
	dīvīsor: dīvīsōrem	*divisor (agent hired to distribute bribes)*
	dīxit	*said*
	docet: docuit	*teaches*
	doctus	*skilful, experienced*
	dolet	*hurts, is in pain*
	domina	*lady (of the household)*
2	dominus	*master (of the household)*
	dōnum	*present, gift*
2	dormit: dormīvit	*sleeps*
	dubium	*doubt*
8	dūcit: dūxit	*leads, takes*
	in mātrimōnium dūxit	*married*
12	duo	*two*

e

4	ē	*from, out of*
	eam	*her, it*
	eās	*them*
	ēbrius	*drunk*
4	ecce!	*look!*
	ēdit	*presents*
	effūgit	*escaped*
4	ego	*I*
4	ēheu!	*oh dear! oh no!*
	ēlēgit	*chose*
6	emit: ēmit	*buys*
9	ēmittit: ēmīsit	*throws out, sends out*
	eōs	*them*
12	epistula	*letter*

	ērāsit	*removed, erased*
	erat	*was*
	ērubēscit	*blushes*
1	est	*is*
	ēsurit	*is hungry*
3	et	*and*
	euge!	*hurray!*
8	eum	*him, it*
	ēvānuit	*vanished*
	ēvītāvit	*avoided*
	ēvolāvit	*flew*
	ex	*from, out of*
	exanimātus	*unconscious*
	excitāvit	*woke up, roused*
10	exclāmat: exclāmāvit	*exclaims, shouts out*
	exercet	*exercises*
	sē exercet	*takes exercise*
3	exit	*goes out*
	expedītus	*lightly armed*
	explicāvit	*explained*
3	exspectat	*waits for*
	exspīrāvit	*died*
	extrāxit	*pulled out*

f

5	fābula	*play, story*
	fābulam agit	*acts out a play*
	fābulam dat	*puts on a play*
8	facile	*easily*
7	facit: fēcit	*makes, does*
	familia	*household*
	fautor: fautōrem	*supporter*
11	favet: fāvit	*favours, supports*
7	fēcit	*made, did*
	fēlēs: fēlem	*cat*
	fēlīx: fēlīcem	*lucky, fortunate*
5	fēmina	*woman*
6	ferōciter	*fiercely*
8	ferōx: ferōcem	*fierce, ferocious*
	ferōcissimus	*very fierce*
9	fert: tulit	*brings, carries*
6	festīnat: festīnāvit	*hurries*

	fidēlis	faithful, loyal
1	fīlia	daughter
1	fīlius	son
	fīnis: fīnem	end
12	flamma	flame
	fluit	flows
	follis: follem	punchball
	fortasse	perhaps
6	fortis	brave, strong
	fortior	braver
	fortissimus	very brave
12	fortiter	bravely
4	forum	forum (marketplace)
	frāctus	broken
10	frāter: frātrem	brother
12	frūstrā	in vain
12	fugit: fūgit	runs away, flees
	fugitīvus	fugitive (from slavery)
	fūmus	smoke
	fūnambulus	tightrope walker
12	fundus	farm
6	fūr: fūrem	thief
	furcifer	scoundrel, rascal
	fūstis: fūstem	club, stick

g

	garrit	chatters, gossips
	gēns: gentem	family
	gerit	wears
	gladiātor: gladiātōrem	gladiator
8	gladius	sword
	Graecia	Greece
	Graeculus	poor little Greek
	Graecus	Greek
	grātiae	thanks
	grātiās agit	thanks, is grateful
	graviter	seriously
	gustat: gustāvit	tastes

h

4	habet	has
10	habitat: habitāvit	lives

	hae	these
	haec	this
	hanc	this
	hausit	drained
	hercle!	by Hercules! good heavens!
7	herī	yesterday
8	hic	this
	hoc	this
5	hodiē	today
9	homō: hominem	person, human being, man
1	hortus	garden
9	hospes: hospitem	guest
	hūc	here, to this place
	hunc	this

i

12	iacet: iacuit	lies, rests
12	iam	now
	iamprīdem	a long time ago
3	iānua	door
	ībat	was going
	ibi	there
11	igitur	therefore, and so
8	ignāvus	cowardly, lazy
	illam	that
9	ille	that
	imitātor: imitātōrem	imitator
	immōtus	still, motionless
10	imperium	empire
	impetus	attack
	imprimit	presses
	impūne	safely
1	in	in, on; into, onto
	incendium	blaze, fire
	incidit: incidit	falls
	incitat: incitāvit	urges on, encourages
	induit	puts on
	īnfāns: īnfantem	child, baby
	īnfēlīx: īnfēlīcem	unlucky
7	ingēns: ingentem	huge

	inimīcus	*enemy*
4	inquit: inquit	*says*
	īnsānus	*mad, crazy*
	īnscrīptiō: īnscrīptiōnem	*writing, inscription*
9	īnspicit: īnspexit	*examines, inspects*
	īnsula	*block of flats*
7	intellegit: intellēxit	*understands*
	rem intellegit	*understands the truth*
6	intentē	*closely, carefully*
	interfēcit	*killed*
2	intrat: intrāvit	*enters*
	intus	*inside*
10	invenit: invēnit	*finds*
11	invītat: invītāvit	*invites*
3	īrātus	*angry*
	īrātior	*angrier*
	īrātissimus	*very angry*
	iste	*that*
11	it: iit	*goes*
	ita	*in this way*
	ita vērō	*yes*
	iter	*journey, progress*
9	iterum	*again*
	iubet	*orders*
	iūdex: iūdicem	*judge*
5	iuvenis: iuvenem	*young person*

l

1	labōrat	*works*
7	lacrimat: lacrimāvit	*cries, weeps*
	laetē	*happily*
2	laetus	*happy*
	laetissimus	*very happy*
	lambit	*licks*
	lapideus	*made of stone*
	larārium	*lararium (shrine of household gods)*
	larēs	*Lares (household gods)*
	Latīnus	*Latin*
	lātrat: lātrāvit	*barks*
2	laudat: laudāvit	*praises*

	lectus	*couch*
11	legit: lēgit	*reads*
8	leō: leōnem	*lion*
10	liber: librum	*book*
11	līberālis	*generous*
	līberālissimus	*very generous*
	līberāvit	*freed, set free*
	līberī	*children*
	līberta	*freedwoman, ex-slave (female)*
6	lībertus	*freedman, ex-slave (male)*
	lingua	*language, tongue*
	longē	*far, a long way*
	longus	*long*
	longissimus	*very long*
	lūcet	*shines*
	lūna	*moon*
	lupus	*wolf*

m

	magnificē	*impressively, magnificently*
	magnificus	*impressive, magnificent*
3	magnus	*big, large, great*
	maior	*bigger, larger, greater*
	māne	*in the morning*
9	manet: mānsit	*remains, stays*
	manus	*hand*
	marītus	*husband*
1	māter: mātrem	*mother*
	mātrimōnium	*marriage*
	in mātrimōnium dūxit	*married*
	maximē	*very greatly*
	maximus	*very big, very large, very great*
	mē	*me*
	mēcum	*with me*
9	medius	*middle*
	melior	*better*
	mendācissimus	*very deceitful*
	mendāx: mendācem	*liar*
	mēnsa	*table*

2	mercātor: mercātōrem	*merchant*
5	meus	*my, mine*
	mihi	*to me*
11	minimē!	*definitely not! no!*
12	mīrābilis	*extraordinary, strange*
	miserandus	*pitiful, pathetic*
	missiō: missiōnem	*release*
12	mittit: mīsit	*sends*
12	mōns: montem	*mountain*
	moribundus	*almost dead*
	moritūrus	*going to die*
	mors: mortem	*death*
7	mortuus	*dead*
9	mox	*soon*
5	multus	*much*
5	multī	*many*
	murmillō: murmillōnem	*murmillo (heavily armed gladiator)*
11	mūrus	*(outside) wall*

n

7	nārrat: nārrāvit	*tells, narrates*
	rem nārrāvit	*told the story*
	nāsus	*nose*
	nauta	*sailor*
3	nāvis: nāvem	*ship*
7	necat: necāvit	*kills*
	negōtium	*business*
	negōtium agit	*does business*
	nēmō	*no one, nobody*
7	nihil	*nothing*
	nihil cūrat	*does not care*
	nimium	*too much*
	nisi	*except*
	nōbilis	*noble, of noble birth*
	nōbīs	*to us*
3	nōn	*not*
10	nōs	*we, us*
11	noster: nostrum	*our*
	nōtus	*famous, well known*
	nōtissimus	*very famous, very well known*

	novācula	*razor*
	novus	*new*
	nox: noctem	*night*
	nūbēs: nūbem	*cloud*
	Nūcerīnī	*people of Nuceria*
	nūllus	*no*
	num?	*surely . . . not?*
	numerat	*counts*
	numquam	*never*
11	nunc	*now*
10	nūntiat: nūntiāvit	*announces*
8	nūntius	*messenger*

o

	obdormīvit	*went to sleep*
	occupātus	*busy*
9	offert: obtulit	*offers*
	oleum	*oil*
	olfēcit	*smelled, sniffed*
6	ōlim	*once, some time ago*
7	omnis	*all*
12	optimē	*very well*
5	optimus	*very good, excellent, best*
	ōrātiō: ōrātiōnem	*speech*
	Orcus	*underworld*
	ōrnātrīx: ōrnātrīcem	*hairdresser, stylist*
9	ostendit: ostendit	*shows*
	ōtiōsus	*on holiday, taking time off*

p

12	paene	*nearly, almost*
	palaestra	*palaestra (exercise area)*
	pānis: pānem	*bread*
7	parat: parāvit	*prepares*
	parātus	*ready*
	parce!	*have pity!*
	parēns: parentem	*parent*
	pariēs: parietem	*(internal) wall*
6	parvus	*small, little*
	pāstor: pāstōrem	*shepherd*

1	pater: patrem	*father*
	paulīsper	*for a short time*
	pauper: pauperem	*poor*
	pauperrimus	*very poor*
	pāvō: pāvōnem	*peacock*
	pavor: pavōrem	*panic*
10	pāx: pācem	*peace*
4	pecūnia	*money*
6	per	*through, along*
	percussit	*struck*
	perīculōsus	*dangerous*
	periit	*died, perished*
	personātus	*wearing a mask*
4	perterritus	*terrified*
	pervēnit	*reached, arrived*
8	pēs: pedem	*paw, foot*
	pessimus	*very bad*
	pestis: pestem	*pest, nuisance*
5	petit: petīvit	*makes for, heads for, attacks*
	philosophus	*philosopher*
	pictūra	*painting, picture*
	pingit	*paints*
	piscīna	*fish pond*
	pistor: pistōrem	*baker*
11	placet: placuit	*it pleases, it suits*
5	plaudit: plausit	*applauds, claps*
	plēnus	*full*
	plūrimus	*most*
	pōculum	*cup*
	poēta	*poet*
	pollex: pollicem	*thumb*
	Pompēiānus	*Pompeian*
	pōns: pontem	*bridge*
8	porta	*gate*
3	portat: portāvit	*carries*
	porticus	*colonnade*
10	portus	*harbour*
9	post	*after, behind*
	posteā	*afterwards*
6	postquam	*after, when*
	postrēmō	*finally, lastly*

	postrīdiē	*(on) the next day*
8	postulat: postulāvit	*demands*
	posuit	*put up, placed*
	praemium	*reward, prize*
	pretiōsus	*precious, expensive*
11	prīmus	*first*
	probat	*proves*
	rem probat	*proves the case*
	probus	*honest*
9	prōcēdit: prōcessit	*advances, proceeds*
11	prōmittit: prōmīsit	*promises*
7	prope	*near*
	prōvocāvit	*challenged*
	proximus	*nearest*
5	puella	*girl*
8	puer: puerum	*boy*
	pugil: pugilem	*boxer*
11	pugna	*fight*
8	pugnat: pugnāvit	*fights*
9	pulcher: pulchrum	*beautiful, handsome*
	pulchrior	*more beautiful, more handsome*
	pulcherrimus	*very beautiful, very handsome*
6	pulsat: pulsāvit	*knocks at, hits, punches*
	pȳramis: pȳramidem	*pyramid*

q

	quadrāgintā	*forty*
4	quaerit: quaesīvit	*looks for, searches for*
10	quam	*than; how*
	quam celerrimē	*as quickly as possible*
	quantī?	*how much?*
	quid?	*what?*
	quiētus	*quiet*
	quīndecim	*fifteen*
	quīnquāgintā	*fifty*
	quīnque	*five*
4	quis?	*who?*
	quō?	*where (to)?*
6	quod	*because*
2	quoque	*also, too*

r

	rādit	scrapes
	rapuit	seized, grabbed
	recitat: recitāvit	recites
	recumbit: recubuit	lies down, reclines
	recūsāvit	refused
4	reddit	gives back
	rediit	went back, returned
6	rēs: rem	thing, matter
	rem intellegit	understands the truth
	rem nārrāvit	told the story
	rem probat	proves the case
	respīrāvit	recovered consciousness
3	respondet: respondit	replies
	rētiārius	retiarius (gladiator with a net)
	retinet	holds back, keeps (back)
9	revenit: revēnit	comes back, returns
	rhētor: rhētorem	teacher
3	rīdet: rīsit	laughs, smiles
	rīdiculus	ridiculous, laughable
7	rogat: rogāvit	asks
	Rōma	Rome
	Rōmānus	Roman
	ruīna	ruin, wreckage
	ruit: ruit	rushes

s

	sacrificium	sacrifice, offering
8	saepe	often
	salit	jumps, leaps
	salūs: salūtem	safety
2	salūtat: salūtāvit	greets
3	salvē!	hello!
8	sanguis: sanguinem	blood
4	satis	enough
	scaena	stage
	scissus	torn
	scit	knows
6	scrībit	writes
	scrīptor: scrīptōrem	signwriter
	sculptor: sculptōrem	sculptor
	scurrīlis	rude, vulgar
	sē exercet	takes exercise
	secat	cuts
	secundus	second
4	sed	but
3	sedet	sits
	sella	chair
	sēmirutus	half collapsed
	sēmisomnus	half asleep
10	semper	always
11	senātor: senātōrem	senator
5	senex: senem	old man
	senior	older
	sēnsim	gradually, slowly
	sententia	opinion
12	sentit: sēnsit	feels
	serpēns: serpentem	snake
10	servat: servāvit	saves, keeps (safe), looks after
1	servus	(male) slave, enslaved man
	sibi	to himself, to herself
8	signum	seal, signal, sign
8	silva	wood, forest
	sine	without
11	sollicitus	troubled, anxious
10	sōlus	alone, lonely
	sonuit	sounded
	sonus	sound
	sordidus	dirty, filthy
	soror: sorōrem	sister
	spectāculum	spectacle, show
5	spectat: spectāvit	looks at, watches
	spectātor: spectātōrem	spectator
	spīna	thorn
	splendidus	splendid
5	stat	stands
8	statim	at once
	statua	statue
	stēlla	star

	stertit	*snores*
	stola	*(long) dress*
	strigil: strigilem	*strigil, scraper*
11	stultus	*foolish*
	stultior	*more foolish*
	stultissimus	*very foolish*
	suāviter	*sweetly*
6	subitō	*suddenly*
	sunt	*are*
6	superat: superāvit	*overcomes, overpowers*
	superfuit	*survived*
7	surgit: surrēxit	*gets up, rises*
	suscipit	*undertakes, takes on*
	susurrāvit	*whispered, muttered*
10	suus	*his, her, their*

t

3	taberna	*shop, inn*
	tablīnum	*study*
10	tacet: tacuit	*is silent, is quiet*
7	tacitē	*quietly, silently*
7	tamen	*however*
12	tandem	*at last*
	tantum	*only*
	tē	*you (singular)*
	tēcum	*with you (singular)*
12	templum	*temple*
	tenet	*holds*
	tepidārium	*warm room*
12	terra	*ground, land*
7	terret: terruit	*frightens*
	tertius	*third*
	testis: testem	*witness*
	theātrum	*theatre*
	thermae	*baths*
	tibi	*to you (singular)*
12	timet: timuit	*is afraid (of), fears*
	timidē	*nervously*
	titulus	*notice, slogan*
	toga	*toga*
	tondet	*shaves, trims*
	tōnsor: tōnsōrem	*barber*

8	tōtus	*whole*
9	trādit: trādidit	*hands over*
	trahit: trāxit	*drags*
	tremor: tremōrem	*earth tremor*
	tremuit	*trembled, shook*
12	trēs	*three*
	trīclīnium	*dining room*
	trīgintā	*thirty*
	trīstis	*sad*
	trīstissimus	*very sad*
4	tū	*you (singular)*
	tuba	*trumpet*
6	tum	*then*
	tunica	*tunic*
5	turba	*crowd*
	turbulentus	*unruly, disruptive*
	tūtus	*safe*
6	tuus	*your, yours*

u

5	ubi	*where*
	ubīque	*everywhere*
	ululāvit	*howled*
	umbra	*ghost, shadow*
12	ūnus	*one*
5	urbs: urbem	*city*
	ūtilis	*useful*
	ūtilissimus	*very useful*
10	uxor: uxōrem	*wife*

v

	vāgīvit	*wailed*
7	valdē	*very much, very*
11	valē	*goodbye*
10	vehementer	*loudly, energetically*
	vēnābulum	*hunting spear*
	vēnālīcius	*slave dealer*
	vēnātiō: vēnātiōnem	*hunt*
6	vēndit: vēndidit	*sells*
5	venit: vēnit	*comes*
11	verberat: verberāvit	*strikes, beats*
	versipellis: versipellem	*werewolf*

Index of grammatical topics

Index of cultural topics

Acknowledgements

This edition of the Cambridge Latin Course (CLC) is the result of over fifty years of research, classroom testing, feedback, revision and development. During that period millions of students, tens of thousands of teachers, hundreds of experts in the fields of Classics, History and Education, and dozens of authors have contributed to make the CLC the success that it is today. To list everyone who has played a part would be impossible, but particular thanks are due to the following individuals for their work on this fifth edition of Book I.

All team members – past and present – at the Cambridge School Classics Project (CSCP), without whom this course simply would not exist. A special mention is due to Lisa Hay for her outstanding dedication and work on this edition.

All the teachers and collaborators who took the time to review our materials and offer helpful feedback and suggestions.

Ben Harris for his crucial authorial input and generous sharing of expertise.

James Watson for his critical eye and attention to detail.

Lottie Mortimer for her work on the cultural background sections.

The following individuals who undertook academic reviews of the material: Thomas Matthew Boehmer, Olivia Elder, Ingo Gildenhard, Sophie Hay and Sophie Wardle.

John Bracey, Tom Di Giulio and Miriam Patrick for their critical friendship and expertise. Jasmine Elmer, Bet Hucks and Pria Jackson for their important and insightful reviews.

And finally, the CSCP team would like to thank our Director, Caroline Bristow, for her ever-enthusiastic and collaborative leadership. Her energy has carried this project from strength to strength and produced a new, vibrant and inclusive CLC edition for the waiting Classics community.

The authors and publishers acknowledge the following sources of copyright material and are grateful for the permissions granted. While every effort has been made, it has not always been possible to identify the sources of all the material used, or to trace all copyright holders. If any omissions are brought to our notice, we will be happy to include the appropriate acknowledgements on reprinting. Thanks to the following for permission to reproduce images:

Cover photo DEA/G. Nimatallah/De Agostini/GI (repeated pp1 & 9*br*); *Inside* pp6, 9*t*, 12*t*, 13, 32*b*, 40, 41, 44*t*, 51, 61*(2)*, 110*tr*, 151*t*, 152*t*, 163, 181, 183, 187, 206*r*, 202*r*, 206, 2011 Roger Dalladay; p7 DEA/Archivio J. Lange/ De Agostini/GI; p9*tl, tr* Su concessione del Ministero della Cultura - Museo Archeologico Nazionale di Napoli; p12*b* DE Agostini Picture Library/GI; p14*l* Alex Saren; p14*r* Larisa Shpineva/GI; pp15, 16 © Jackie and Bob Dunn www.pompeiiinpictures.com Su concessione del MiC - Parco Archeologico di Pompei; p17 Mario Laporta/AFP/GI; pp18, 55, 64*(4)* DEA/L. Romano/De Agostini/GI; pp19, 28*r*,32*t* Werner Forman/GI; pp25, 32*c*, 113*cl*, 117*b*, 133 *(neck guard, greave)*, 147, 148, 152*b*, 156 CSCP; p27 Christophel Fine Art/ GI; p28*l* PHAS/GI; p28*cl* DEA Picture Library/ De Agostini/GI; p28*cr,b*, 34, 38*tl*, 46*l,br*, 47*tr*, 65*(9)*, 79*l*, 81*(1&2)*, 83, 93, 126, 128, 134, 135, 139, 146, 189*t* DEA/A. Dagli Orti/De Agostini/GI; p29 © Mariano De Angelis; p30 Su concessione del Ministero della Cultura - Parc Archeologico di Pompei, further use of